# Well-Done Roasts

# Well-Done Roasts

### Witty Insults, Quips & Wisecracks
### Perfect for Every Imaginable Occasion

By William R. Evans III

Andrew Frothingham

St. Martin's Press
New York

**To the idiot with whom I wrote this book.**

Production Editor: David Stanford Burr

Library of Congress Cataloging-in-Publication Data

Frothingham, Andrew.
    Well-done roasts : witty insults, quips & wisecracks perfect
for every imaginable occasion / Andrew Frothingham and William R.
Evans III.
        p.   cm.
    "A Thomas Dunne book."
    ISBN 0-312-08334-3
    1. Roasts (Public speaking)   I. Evans, Tripp.   II. Title.
PN4193.R63F76   1992
808.5′1—dc20                                                92-26158
                                                                CIP

First Edition: November 1992

10 9 8 7 6 5 4 3

3 4873 00147 1127

# TABLE OF CONTENTS

# LIST OF SYNONYMS

ix

# INTRODUCTION

Oh no!. You've been asked to take part in a roast!. You have to come up with some sensationally scathing bits of dirt about a friend, a co-worker, a boss, or a loved one. Don't panic—most roasts include several roasters, so your time to speak will be short and you'll only need a few choice comments. This book provides thousands of roasts—insults, affronts, slights, snubs—of varying intensity. They can be used on everyone from the chairman of the board to an old drinking buddy.

If you happen to find yourself the target of honor, this book will not only prepare you, it also includes a section of great snappy comebacks. For example: *When you told me you were going to roast me I thought, Naturally, they only crucify the innocent*. (See "ROASTEES," page 3.)

# HOW TO USE THIS BOOK

*Well-Done Roasts* is an up-to-date, user-friendly, nonsexist manual for today's busy executive, entertainer, host, or honoree. Locating that ideal zinger is a snap. Just find out a few facts about the intended target and turn to the Table of Contents or List of Synonyms in the front of the book. For example, you'll find golf under SPORTS on page 125; BOSSES, BAD is on page 36. You'll also find comments about WIMPS (page 143), LOSERS (page 74), and UNCOUTH (page 139). Both adjectives and nouns are included, so don't worry about grammar, just look up the first words that come to mind. If the category you're interested in doesn't appear on the Contents page, check out the List of Synonyms.

(If you're looking for a roast about parenthood, the synonym list will direct you to FAMILY. All categories in the book are in upper case; synonyms are in lower case. Some roasts appear in more than one category, so you don't have to fumble around the book chasing cross-reference footnotes. The line, *He's still chasing women, but he can't remember why,* is listed under AGE, OLD (page 5) *and* under OLD MEN, DIRTY (page 92).

Don't treat the material in this book as sacred. Feel free to change the him in an insult to her, and vice versa. Better yet, use your target's name. Don't say, *He thinks* innuendo *is an Italian suppository* (page 134), say, *Dan isn't real smart—he thinks* . . . Do, however, treat the book itself as sacred. Don't loan it to other people. This is in your best interests, as it keeps ammunition away from people who might use it on you.

# SOME SUGGESTIONS

- Select a few more roasts than you think you'll need; you never know when a roaster who precedes you will use one of your lines.
- Being roasted is an honor—it's a sign of affection and admiration. If you're roasting a friend, show no mercy. Tell every embarrassing story you know about her. Dredge up her humiliating fifth-grade nickname.
- Conversely, if you're asked to roast someone whom you're not that close to, you may want to steer clear from the really biting comments. One good way to soften an insult is to put it into the past. Don't say, *He's so conceited, he has his X-rays retouched* (page 53), say *He used to be so conceited, he'd get his X-rays retouched.*
- Another good tactic is to include yourself in the roast. Instead of saying, *He's so cheap, he buys reversible condoms* (page 40), say, *He's almost as cheap as I am; he buys reversible condoms.*
- If you can't think of a particular incident with which to embarrass the guest of honor, consider some general categories. For instance, everybody has a home town (*She comes from cattle country, where they teach 'em how to throw bull at an early age.*), an occupation (psychia-

trists/psychologists: *He practices a new kind of shock therapy—he sends his bill in advance*), or a hobby (*He had to take steroids to be on the chess team*). How about her apperance? Is she fat? (Ex: *She's so heavy, she can't get out of bed in the morning, because she keeps rocking herself back to sleep*.) Tall? (Ex: *He's so tall, it brings new meaning to the phrase* the height of stupidity.) Large breasted? (Ex: *Midgets stand under her for shelter during storms*.) Bald? (Ex: *He combs his hair with a sponge*.) There's always something you can make fun of, and that's the point: Have fun.

- If you have no time at all to prepare, you can always use one of the classic roast or roastee lines in the sections following this introduction.

# THE PRICE OF SUCCESS

This book gives you all the material you need to give biting, irreverent roasts. If, however, you get a reputation for giving scintillating and profane roasts, you'll probably get invited to participate in a toast or deliver a speech. To prepare for those occasions, you'll want to pick up a copy of *CRISP TOASTS—Wonderful Words That Add Wit and Class Every Time You Raise Your Glass* or *AND I QUOTE—The Definitive Collection of Quotes, Sayings, and Jokes for the Contemporary Speechmaker*. Both are published by St. Martin's Press.

# Well-Done Roasts

# ROASTS

- There's no way this roast will make an ass out of him—nature did that long ago.

- There are many things you could say about her. That she's modest, kind, bright, and polite. They'd all be lies, but you could say them.

- Why should I be nice? The fool came here to be roasted, and, as Pierre Corneille said, "He who allows himself to be insulted deserves to be."

- In my book she's a great lady; but my book is fiction.

- He's a true friend; like John Barrymore. His last words to his friend Gene Fowler were "Tell me, Gene, is it true that you are the illegitimate son of Buffalo Bill?"

- It's great to be asked to be part of this roast. I really like [name], but I feel she needs a little deflating now and then. I guess I feel the way Jack Paar felt about Steve Allen when he said, "I'm fond of Steve Allen, but not as much as he is."

- He's modest, but, as Winston Churchill once said about Clement Atlee, "He has much to be modest about."

- It's appropriate that we give her a dinner; everyone does. She hasn't picked up a check in years.

- You're not much of a go-getter. Let me give you a piece of advice: Remember the words of Sophie Tucker who said, "I have been poor and I have been rich. Rich is better."

- At first, we were going to do a normal testimonial dinner, instead of a roast. But she begged us to roast her. She said if her husband ever heard how much we really liked her, he'd never forgive her for not getting more pay and a better title.

- They wanted to have him roasted by a close friend—but they couldn't find one, so I came instead.

- We wanted to give her something she really needs, but we couldn't figure out how to wrap a bathtub.

- We thought it would be good to get together and say nice things about her—but then we decided to tell the truth, so we are having this roast.

- A lot of nice things have been said about you tonight: Your friends are either very dumb or very good liars.

- I'm not sure why we decided to give him such a great going-away party: Maybe to let him know how much we appreciate all he's done; maybe to keep him quiet.

- We wanted to give him a piece of the office. We clearly can't give him the elevator, but we can always give him the shaft.

- Her employees threw her a big dinner. Unfortunately, it didn't hit her.

- His wife is delighted that he's here today. While he's away, she's having his cage cleaned.

- You've got to give the woman credit. She's the only one I know who's dumb enough to come to this little gathering with an open mind, a complete lack of prejudice, and a cool willingness to hear the rubbish we're about to dump on her.

- What can you say about our guest of honor that hasn't been said about hazardous waste?

- She's humble and modest—and she has good reason to be.

- Ladies and gentlemen, I give you our guest of honor—and you can have him.

- I'm proud to be here to honor her. I love her. I have no taste, but I love her.

- The chairman would have been here, except for the distance: He's in the lobby.

- I can only give our friend here one piece of advice, and it comes from that great American philosopher W. C. Fields: "If at first you don't succeed, try, try again. Then give up. No use being a damn fool about it."

# ROASTEES

- So you're going to try and roast me. Well, in the words of that Pat Benatar song, "Hit me with your best shot, fire away."

- I came to this event knowing that you would seek to injure me with your wordplay, but I am not afraid. Why? Because I'm protected by a mantra that was passed on to me by my wise ancestors. It goes like this: "Stick and stones may break my bones, but names will never hurt me. Nay-nay-a-boo-boo."

- So, I am to be roasted. I guess that's what happens to a big ham.

- I thought I was going to be roasted. Hah! You people don't have enough fire power to roast a peanut.

- To all those who wish to roast me, I have just one piece of advice. Remember that when you point a finger, three fingers are pointing back at you.

- Before you make your comments too biting, remember I'm the vengeful type. How much rest do you think you'll get sleeping with one eye open?

- I know I'm no raving beauty. I have a lot in common with Phyllis Diller who said, "Sometimes I just go to the beauty parlor for an estimate."

- Before you begin to roast me, think of what I know about you. Think of the *years* we've worked together. I know where the bodies are buried.

- When I look at this fine collection of friends gathered here to insult me, I can only think of Julius Caesar's last words: *Et tu, Brute?*

3

- When you told me you were going to roast me, I thought, *Naturally, they only crucify the innocent.*

- I take the fact that you are going to roast me as a sign of my success and your incredible jealousy. Ambrose Bierce said it best when he defined success as "the one unpardonable sin against one's fellows."

- I'm not sure how to respond to being roasted. It seems sacrilegious, but my first reaction is to quote Jesus who said, "Forgive them: They know not what they do."

- Looking around at this roast, I am reminded of David Evans, a nineteenth-century murderer, whose last words before being executed were "There are worse men here than me."

- Talk about me, but not about my family: I belong to the Fred Allen school of ancestry and its motto is "I don't want to look up my family tree because I know I'm the sap."

- I'll admit I'm from a small town. You know how the big cities have professional call girls? In our little town, we had to make do with volunteers.

- If you are going to roast me, keep it fair. Don't, for example, make a big thing about the fact that I go out with younger women. I have to. As George Burns said, "All the women my age are dead."

# ABSENTMINDEDNESS

- She's so absent minded she can hide her own Easter eggs.
- Okay, I'll admit his absent mindedness borders on Alzheimer's. But that's not such a negative—think of all the new people he's constantly meeting.
- She's a true friend. I can call her at any hour of the night and pour my heart out and be sure that she won't remember a thing in the morning.
- The only thing that can stay in her head more than an hour is a cold.

- His health is endangered when you lend him money—it damages his memory.

- I don't understand what's the big deal. He might be getting a little older, but he's not losing his mind. In fact, just the other day he exclaimed in a loud, robust voice, "I've got my health, my heart is strong, my liver is good, and my mind, knock wood. . . . Who's there?"

# AGE, OLD

- Bob Hope was most diplomatic when discussing the white lies many of us tell about how old we are. I think he had our guest of honor in mind when he remarked, "She said she was approaching forty, and I couldn't help wondering from what direction."

- He never lies about his age. He just tells everyone he's as old as his wife. Then he lies about *her* age.

- I'm the most dangerous person in the room for [name]. Because I knew her long ago, before she became so respectable. It's like what Groucho Marx once said about Doris Day: "I've been around so long, I knew Doris Day before she was a virgin."

- She's so old, the birthday candles cost more than the cake.

- As you've probably noticed, the candles on his cake are not a true representation of the birthday boy's age. We tried to put the exact number of candles on the cake, but by the time we had lit the last one, the first ones were a puddle of wax.

- I don't think you all appreciate how old this woman is today. She's so old that when she was in school, history was current events.

- Hey, the guy's not that old. Give him a break. I know for a fact he still chases girls—unfortunately, it's only downhill.

- The poor guy's getting old, all right. How do I know? Well, just the other day he told me that his wife had given up sex for Lent and he didn't find out till Easter.

5

- I don't understand what's the big deal. She might be getting a little older, but she's not losing her mind. In fact, just the other day she exclaimed in a loud, robust voice, "I've got my health, my heart is strong, my liver is good, and my mind, knock wood . . . Who's there?"

- Getting old is not all bad. Just think, you won't be bothered by insurance salespeople any more.

- He's in great shape. He reminds me of Gore Vidal's description of Ronald Reagan as "a triumph of the embalmer's art."

- If I might borrow a quote from the great wit, Oscar Wilde, "He is old enough to know worse."

- She's so old her social security number is 7.

- He was going to get a vasectomy, but the doctor said to let sleeping dogs lie.

- At his age, his back goes out more than he does.

- He's an old guy, like George Burns, and, as Jackie Gleason once described Burns, "George reads *Playboy* for the same reason he reads *National Geographic*—to see places he'll never get to visit."

- Elbert Hubbard summed it up best about our guest of honor when he said, "Boys will be boys, and so will a lot of middle-aged men."

- She goes out with younger men—at her age, there are no older men.

- As she ages, she keeps everything in perspective. For example, as Diane de Poitiers said, "The years that a woman subtracts from her age are not lost. They are added to the ages of other women."

- At his age, when a woman flirts with him in the movies, she's after his popcorn.

- Look at her. In all these years she hasn't lost a thing. In fact, she's like Lucille Ball who said, "I have everything I had twenty years ago—only it's all a little bit lower."

- He's always complaining about getting old. He should remember Maurice Chevalier's comment that "Old age isn't so bad when you consider the alternative."

- He's so old he can remember a pro boxing match between two white guys.

- Everyone tonight has told you how great you look. Don't let it go to your head. Cardinal Spellman once identified the "three ages of man: youth, age, and 'you are looking wonderful.'"

- At her age, when she goes to bed, she turns out the lights to save money, not to fool around.

- Given his age, when he makes a donation in church, it's not a donation, it's an investment.

- If I knew I was going to become a crabby old person like her, I'd kill myself now.

- At his age, when he goes out with a girl, he can't take yes for an answer.

- He's not aging with the same style as his wife. That's to be expected. As Helen Rowland said, "Nowadays, most women grow old gracefully; most men, disgracefully."

- She looks like a million dollars—all green and wrinkled.

- He always goes out with younger women—he believes that you are only as old as the person you are feeling.

- She's getting cautious in her old age—she now slows down for stoplights.

- I've got socks older than she is.

- The guy's amazing. Robert Frost described his type perfectly when he said, "He forgets his wife's birthday, but he remembers her age."

- She knows her mind. When she reached forty, she definitely decided what she wanted to be—thirty-five.

- She'll admit she's pushing forty, but most of us would agree that she's not really pushing it, she's dragging it.

7

- He's still chasing women, but he can't remember why.
- At his age, all women look the same—good.
- At seventy years of age, his greatest ambition is to be shot by a jealous husband at eighty.
- She never forgets her age, once she's decided what it's to be.
- The best years of her life were the ten years between twenty-nine and thirty.
- When the census taker asked her how old she was, she couldn't remember whether she was forty-two or forty-three, so she said thirty-five.
- In her opinion, the seven ages of a woman are: baby, infant, junior miss, young woman, young woman, young woman, young woman.
- You can tell he's getting old—when he propositions a girl, he hopes she says no.
- At his age, he's more interested in hearing yes from a banker than from a blonde in a bikini.
- The only thing she grows in her garden is tired.
- He's begun to have *thoughts* about women instead of *feelings*.
- His head makes dates that his body can't keep.
- That little voice in his head that used to say "Why not?" now usually says, "Why bother?"
- She breaks all the rules . . . like the one that says that wisdom comes with age.
- She looks like a million . . . every day of it.
- He's eighty-two years old, but he often feels like a twenty-six-year-old; not that he ever gets one.
- Sometimes I question the true age of our guest of honor. As Oscar Wilde noted, "Thirty-five is a very attractive age. London society is full of women of the very highest birth who have, of their own free choice, remained thirty-five for years."

# ANCESTRY, QUESTIONABLE

- He comes from a family of standing. They all worked behind the counter at McDonalds.

- She said she wanted to see her family, so I took her to the zoo.

- Her baby is descended from a long line that she listened to.

- People like him don't just grow on trees—they swing from them.

- One of his ancestors was a famous king . . . King Kong.

- In an old, distinguished family tree, she's the sap.

- He likes to steer clear of any talk about his family history. In fact, he'd be the first to agree with Fred Allen who said, "I don't want to look up my family tree because I know I'm the sap."

- He's trying to get from the cash register to the social register.

- The only thing she can do well is inherit.

- She claims she came over on the *Mayflower*—thank God the immigration laws are much stricter now.

# APPEARANCE, APPALLING

## Acne

- In her youth, she had such a bad case of acne, a blind man could read her face.

- Those aren't acne scars on his face; he just had a hard time learning to eat with a fork.

- When she was a teenager, she was the poster girl for the American Pizza Association.

- He has the face of a famous general: Manuel Norreiga.
- His face has more craters than the moon.
- She has a *Great Escape* face: It's always breaking out.

## Baldness

- He proves the statement: hair today, gone tomorrow.
- He combs his hair with a sponge.
- It's not that he's bald headed—he just has a tall face.
- His hair isn't all gone: Some of it is in a drawer in his bedroom.

## Beards

- Most men's mothers say, "You have such a nice face; why grow a beard and cover it?" His didn't.
- They say that men who grow beards have something to hide . . .
- His wife doesn't have to ask him what he had for lunch—she just looks at his beard.
- He looks like he's trying out for a ZZ Top look-alike contest.
- His beard keeps him from being a bald-faced liar.
- Maybe that's a beard on his face—but maybe he swallowed a beaver.

## Body

- Anatomy is something every woman has, but on her it doesn't look so good.
- She has everything a man would desire, including heft, bulging muscles, and a moustache.

- He once asked his physician if he should undergo a sex-change operation, and the doctor said, "From what?"
- For years, we've watched her growth, hoping she'd have it removed.
- I heard he was arrested the other day for indecent exposure. Luckily, he got off on a technicality; lack of evidence.
- She left her body to science, but science wouldn't take it.
- A peeping Tom reached in and pulled down her window shade.
- She has long black hair—and wears gloves to hide it.
- At his age, his back goes out more than he does.

# Breasts

*busty-chested*

- Midgets stand under her for shelter during storms.
- If she falls over, she won't break her nose.
- Her babies have stretchmarks on their lips.
- She's a real up-front girl.

*droopy-chested*

- You know the pencil test? She could hold a dictionary.
- If she doesn't wear a bra, she trips.
- She wore a minidress last week and her nipples showed.

*flat-chested*

- She has the smallest boobs in this office—and that's counting the men.
- She has bras that are strapless *and* cupless.

- She's a carpenter's dream—flat as a board and easy to screw.

- She's a pirate's dream—sunken chest.

- There's enough cotton in her bra to start a new chapter of the Red Cross.

## Ears

- He sometimes says he can't believe his ears—I can't either.

- When she says, "I'm all ears," you believe her.

- He really, *really* associated with Dumbo.

- Her ears are so big that her head looks like a loving cup.

- "Does he have big ears?" you ask. Well, last time he was in a restaurant, five people hung their hats on them.

## Eyes

- She always has a blank stare. Who says you can't tell a woman's mind by her eyes?

- He's got brown eyes—another proof that he's full of shit.

- Sure her eyes are always watering. She has to smell her own breath.

- His eyes are a bit shifty. He went to an ophthalmologist and the doctor got motion sickness.

- Only her red, bloodshot eyes keep her from being entirely colorless.

## Face

- Her face is—let's be polite—unusual. It's the kind of face that inspired Groucho Marx to say, "I never forget a face, but in your case I'll make an exception."

- The only funny lines he has are on his face.
- She went to the Tammy Faye Bakker cosmetics school.
- Her family is very protective of her . . . they don't let her out on garbage-collection day.
- He was made for radio—he's much too ugly to be seen.
- Her photographs do her an injustice—they look just like her.
- When women kiss him they always close their eyes: They have to.
- Here's looking at you, though heaven knows it's an effort.
- He was a war baby—his parents took one look at him and started fighting.
- She looks like a movie star . . . Lassie.
- Those aren't acne scars on his face, he just had a hard time learning to eat with a fork.
- He looks like a million dollars—all green and wrinkled.
- Her mother used to warn her not to make stupid faces or her face would get stuck that way. She was right.
- The fact that she's a dead ringer for Monroe has never held her back. Very few people know what our fifth president looked like.
- He has a face like a flower—a cauliflower.
- She looks like a million . . . every day of it.
- Her complexion is like a peach: yellow and fuzzy.
- Beauty is only skin deep—unfortunately, someone peeled her.
- If Moses had seen his face, there would have been another commandment.
- She can't be two-faced. If she had two, why would she be wearing that one?
- He has a face like a saint—a Saint Bernard.
- She looks good after a fashion—after a couple of Old Fashioned.

- He's so ugly, he has to sneak up to the mirror to shave.

- When she comes into a room, the mice jump on chairs.

- He could make a good living renting himself out for Halloween parties.

- He's dark and handsome. When it's dark, he's handsome.

- She was so ugly that the day she was born, her father took one look at her and ran down to the zoo to throw rocks at the stork.

- He looks like an accident going somewhere to happen.

- The only thing that can make her look good is distance.

- She's becoming an emergency-room nurse because she's better off wearing a mask.

- He looks like such an ape that when he goes to the zoo, he needs two tickets; one to get in and one to get out.

- The only time he looks appropriate is on Halloween.

- She has such a sour look that when she puts face cream on, it curdles.

- I hear she once was a beauty. Could have fooled me. I guess, as Craig Nova said, "She's got what I call bobsled looks—going downhill fast."

- I look at her and I want to ask a question once asked by Arthur "Bugs" Baer: "How much would you charge to haunt a house?"

- She's what you call a two-bagger. If you end up going to bed with her, she wears a bag over her head, and you wear one over your head—just in case hers falls off.

- He's coyote ugly. If you find yourself in bed the morning after, and your arm happens to be pinned underneath him, instead of waking him up, you gnaw it off at the elbow and run away.

- She's always been funny. At least as far as looks go.

- As a child, he was so ugly his parents didn't know which end to diaper.

14

- He's so ugly his mother used to tie pork chops around his neck so the dog would play with him.

- If I had a head like that, I'd have it circumcised.

- Her beautician has started talking about mercy killings.

- She has a face like a wedding cake left out in the rain.

- Look at this guy! Jack Kroll summed it up best in his remark about Woody Allen. He has "A face that convinces you that God is a cartoonist."

- Looking at him, I'm reminded of H. Allen Smith's description of Damon Runyon: He's a "mean looking little guy; a statue of him would even scare off pigeons."

- If she lost face, it would be an improvement.

- Whenever I look at her, I'm reminded of a Bette Midler quote: "Princess Anne of England is such an active lass, so outdoorsy—she loves nature in spite of what it did to her."

- She once told me that I was drunk. I came back with Winston Churchill's classic response: "Madame, you're ugly. Tomorrow morning, however, I shall be sober . . ."

- She looked just like she just stepped out of *Vogue* . . . and fell flat on her face.

## Face-lifts

- She's never had her face lifted—they couldn't find a crane large enough.

- She's had her face lifted so many times, she now has a goatee.

- He's had his face lifted so many times there's nothing left inside his shoes.

- She's had so many face-lifts, every time she raises her eyebrows, she pulls up her stockings.
- He's had his face lifted so many times, it's out of focus.
- I heard he had his face lifted because he had more wrinkles than an accordion.
- I heard she was going to have her face lifted. But I couldn't figure out who in the world would want to steal it.

## Fat

- He's so fat, he's one donut away from affecting the tides.
- He always keeps his chins up.
- We're giving him a picture of his toes: We know he hasn't seen them in years.
- Lately, she's become so fashionable. It's nice to see that they're finally putting style into the larger sizes.
- A real candidate for the FBI—the Fat Boys Institute.
- Travel is broadening, and she looks like she's been around the world five times.
- She has a passion for horse shows and she goes whenever she can find a rider.
- At one point, he was so overweight his wife stared at him in amazement and proclaimed, "You're twice the man I married."
- He not only has kept his figure—he's doubled it.
- She doesn't have the figure for a bikini—just the nerve.
- She's too lazy to watch her figure, so the boys don't either.
- Once he asked his son what he plans to do when he's as big as his father. His son answered, "Diet."
- She has to put on a girdle to get into a mumu.

- If he ever gets into an elevator, it had better be going down.

- He's too fat to play golf. If he puts the ball where he can hit it, he can't see it, and if he puts it where he can see it, he can't hit it.

- She was recently on a strict diet—all she lost was her temper.

- He has no trouble at all watching his waistline—it's right there in front where he can see it.

- She has a figure like a pillow.

- He's so fat, his wife gave him a belt for his birthday, and he's using it for a wristband.

- The only well-rounded thing about her is her figure.

- She's like a foreign car—she has all her weight in the rear.

- He's so fat, he eats in a day what most third-world countries eat in a year.

- The girl has a brilliant modeling career ahead of her—as a model for slipcovers.

- He's one guy I love to watch laugh—so much of him has a good time.

- It's not that she's heavy. It's just that when she promenaded down the aisle after the wedding ceremony, the groom had to walk behind her.

- He's so big, he can take a shower without getting his feet wet.

- He's not overweight. He's just ten inches too short.

- The woman's scared of her own shadow—it's beginning to look like a mob.

- He's finding it harder and harder to make ends meet—such as his fingers and toes.

- People say he has no self-control when it comes to eating, but that's not true. There're at least two things he won't eat for dinner, and that's breakfast and lunch.

- She collided with a truck and the truck lost.

- He seems to be trying to eat himself to death. If he does, he can copy

Richard Monckton Milnes whose last words were "My exit is the result of too many entrees."

- I'm reminded of a quote by Mark Twain about Oliver Wendell Holmes. He "had double chins all the way down to his stomach."

- She has an interesting way of aging: She keeps her waistline and her age at the same number.

- Face it, he used to be so big that, as Harpo Marx once said about Alexander Woollcott, "He looked like something that had gotten loose from Macy's Thanksgiving Day Parade."

- Her favorite food? Well, I think Joan Rivers said it best in describing Elizabeth Taylor. She said, "Liz is so fat—her favorite food is seconds."

- I don't think it's fair to call her fat. Let's just say she's just tall around the waist.

- He's so fat that when he gets his shoes shined, he has to take the shoeshiner's word for it.

- She's so big she's the same size whether she stands up or sits down.

- The guy is so fat and out of shape, he looks like Jell-O with a belt.

- He's so fat, he can only play seek.

- She used to be so heavy, she couldn't get out of bed in the morning. She kept rocking herself back to sleep.

- He's so fat he needs shock absorbers on his toilet seat.

- She's so fat if she could jump high she'd cause a solar eclipse.

- He's so fat his bathtub has stretch marks.

- They say old soldiers fade away. Looking at good old [name] over here, it's going to take one hell of a long time before he starts disappearing.

- She's in such awful shape, when she sits down she looks like batter spreading.

- If he were a building, he'd be condemned.

- In the immortal words of Margaret Halsey, "He must have had a magnificent build before his stomach went into a career of its own."

- She's a fat anorectic.

- When Joan Rivers was doing her routine, she came up with some marvelous descriptions for some of her friends. If I hadn't known any better, I would have thought she was talking about our guest of honor. Luckily, I had the presence of mind to copy down some of Ms. Rivers' more memorable lines. Here they are, and I dedicate these to [name of guest of honor]. "She's so fat, she's my two best friends. She wears stretch caftans. She's got more chins than the Chinese."

## Glasses

- She thinks that her glasses are what keep her from getting dates. Let's face it, for her to get a date, all the guys would have to lose *their* glasses.

- He broke his glasses last week. His wife crossed her legs at the wrong moment.

- Of course she wears glasses. You have to put a nose that magnificent to good use.

- He's so blind, he keeps spare glasses so he can find his glasses when he loses them.

- Before she got glasses, she was always having headaches. She still does, but she's going to get rid of her mirror and see if that helps.

## Hair

- He doesn't mind if his hair looks like a mop, especially since he has no idea what a mop looks like.

- Blondes like her do have more fun—so little is expected of them.

19

- She used to have hair all the way down her back—not on her head, just down her back.

- He was mugged by three gay guys—two held him down, and one did his hair.

- She's not really a blonde. She's more like a brunette with a top secret.

- She's dyed her hair so often—her dandruff is technicolored.

- She's a suicide blonde—dyed by her own hand.

- Some women are blond on their mother's side, some on their father's side, but she's blond on the peroxide.

- She's a cross between a brunette and a drugstore.

- She's an established bleachhead.

- No matter how she's feeling, she's always dyeing.

- His hairdo is more like a hair-don't.

## Legs

- With those varicose veins, he could win first prize at a costume party by going as a road map.

- She has the legs of a racehorse—wearing saddlebags.

- I've seen better legs on a piano.

- Her legs are so skinny you can cut yourself on her shins.

- He's got great legs—for a hippo.

- I've seen shapelier stick figures.

## Mouth

- His mouth is so big, he could French-kiss a subway tunnel.

- If she were a fish, she's be a wide-mouthed bass.

- Her mouth is so small, she couldn't go down on a pencil.

- If he opens his mouth in public, people mistake it for a garbage can.
- He has such a big mouth, he can sing a duet by himself.
- His mouth is so big, he can eat a banana sideways.
- She's got such a big mouth, when she yawns, her ears disappear.

## Nose

- She has kept her nose to the grindstone for years—that's one reason why her face looks that way.
- He can't run for president. They couldn't get his nose on a stamp.
- Her nostrils are so big, when you kiss her it's like driving into a two-car garage.
- Of course she wears glasses. You have to put a nose that magnificent to good use.
- Once someone asked if that was his nose or was he eating a banana.
- She has a Roman nose—it roams all over her face.
- Just look at it. His nose is so big, he only has to breathe in once and it lasts all day.
- Her nose is so high in the air, every time she sneezes, she sprays the ceiling.
- Why does he have such a beautiful nose? Well, that's obvious. It's handpicked.
- She has a big nose—and unfortunately, big noses run in her family.
- What a schnozzola—he uses bedsheets for handkerchiefs.
- Why is her nose so big? Air is free.

## Odor, Body

- Body odor? Him? The paint in his office is peeling.
- She's got a definite aroma. She's been known to set off smoke detectors.

- She's an animal—well, at least she smells like one.

- You can tell he's a big cheese—he smells like one.

- Having a locker next to this guy was an ordeal and a half. His feet stunk to high heaven. So one time a couple of us presented him with a package of Odor-Eaters, and you know what happened when he put his shoes on? He disappeared.

## Short

- He's so short that when he pulls his socks up, he can't see where he is going.

- She's so short, she gets winded walking through a shag carpet.

- He's not overweight. He's just ten inches too short.

- I won't say she's tiny, but she'd make a great refrigerator magnet.

- I won't say he's short, but he used to rent himself out as a lawn jockey.

- He wasn't tall enough to become a marine, so they made him a submarine.

- He's short, and maybe that's why he's so weird. It's like Pat McCormick's description of Paul Williams: "Paul's very superstitious. He considers it unlucky to walk under a black cat."

- After hours of extensive research, I finally came across the perfect description of [name] in the form of a Truman Capote quote. Capote, when asked to comment on his own stature, said he was "about as tall as a shotgun, and just about as noisy."

- His favorite exercise is climbing tall women.

- She's as short as Paul Williams, who once claimed to have snuck back into the house through the puppy door after his wife, Katy, locked him out.

- She tried to commit suicide by jumping off a curb.

- He can get into a car without bending over.

- She's so small, she only writes in shorthand.

- He's too often overlooked. That happens when you are a midget.

- Peter Cook said it best when describing Dudley Moore. He said, "You are not very long for this earth. You are, in fact, very short for this earth."

- She sits on two phone books when she drives, so she can see through the steering wheel.

- She's short all right. You know what they'd call her if she were in the Navy? A microwave.

## Tall

- He's so tall, his head is up in the thin air. Maybe lack of oxygen explains how his brain works.

- She's so tall, she can't find guys to go out with that are her height. So her idea of a perfect date is a midget who can kiss well and who has prehensile toes.

- He's so tall that when he drops something on his toes, he doesn't scream until the next day.

- She drives a convertible. She has to, her head won't fit in a normal car.

- He's so tall, it brings new meaning to the phrase *the height of stupidity*.

## Teeth

- He posed as the BEFORE picture in a toothpaste ad.

- She's got a first-class smile—and third-world teeth.

- You could go spelunking in his cavities.

- Her teeth didn't grow that pointed—she had them sharpened.

- His teeth are so stained, he needs to brush them with a power sander.

- She was the original model for the jack-o'-lantern.

- His teeth are his own—he's finally all paid up.

- I've seen better teeth on a comb.

- He's so bucktoothed, he could eat corn through a tennis racket.

## Thin

- She's so thin, she has to be careful not to fall through subway grates.

- Just look at his body. Come on, admit it: You can find better bodies at a used-car lot.

- He's so thin, when he wears black, he resembles a closed umbrella.

- He used to be so thin that when he stood sideways in school, the teacher marked him absent.

- Thin? Are you kidding? She's so thin, she has to jump around in the shower to get wet.

- He's so thin and feeble, when he drinks lemonade through a straw, he has to hold on to a chair to keep from getting sucked back into the glass.

- She's on the Karen Carpenter diet plan.

# ART

## Conducting

- He became a conductor after he failed as a high-class gigolo. It was the only other job where he could use the white tie and tails.

- It's perfect she's a conductor. The audience never has to look at her face.

- Here's to a true conductor—someone who doesn't know how to compose himself.
- She can conduct an orchestra, but she can't conduct herself.

## Music

- We laughed when he sat down, but when he started to play, we cried. It was that bad.
- Her musical education was costly. Her parents were sued by four neighbors.
- Her sound system is a mystery to her—she just doesn't know much about fidelity.
- As Artemus Ward said, "You have Van Gogh's ear for music."
- He's so stupid, he thought Johnny Cash was a pay toilet.
- True, his music has some lovely moments, but as Rossini said about Wagner, it also has "some terrible quarters of an hour."
- She's one of the finest musicians in the country—but in the city she stinks.
- He's not much of a pianist. In fact, Venus de Milo could do better.
- She makes Jack Benny sound good.
- After hearing him, I realize that *violin* and *violence* are related words.
- She was made to be a violin player. Strong arms, long fingers, massive chins.
- He'll never be much of a musician—he never gets past the first two bars.

## Painting

- She says she's an artist, but I don't get it. I'm with Al Capp who defined abstract art as "A product of the untalented, sold by the unprincipled to the utterly bewildered."
- He became an artist because someone told him he could trace the nude model in drawing class.
- Admit it. She's such a dreadful artist, she couldn't even draw a breath.

- The only thing he can draw is a bunch of flies.
- Painting was simply the most *palettable* hobby she could think of.
- He's like his pictures—he should be hung.
- The only thing she knows about art is that it's short for Arthur.

## Sculpting

- She likes sculpting in stone because she enjoys working with something harder than her head.
- His wife asked him to take up sculpting so he'd have something to do with his hands.
- She must be a fine sculptor—everyone is always talking about what a chiseler she is.
- Sculpting is the only time that he puts women on a pedestal.

## Singing

- The only time his voice sounds good is when he gargles.
- I wish she'd just sing Christmas carols; then we'd only have to listen to her once a year.
- His voice is like asthma set to music.
- Her tongue is sharp, but her voice is flat.
- I'm the first to admit he has a fine voice. I just think it's a pity for him to spoil it by singing.
- She couldn't carry a tune in a bucket.
- He had a promising career as a singer, but had to stop to protect his throat . . . people threatened to cut it.
- She sings like a bird—and has a brain like one too.

- He has such a big mouth, he can sing a duet by himself.
- The way she carries a tune, she seems to be staggering under the load.
- His musical education was costly. His parents were sued by four neighbors.
- She's a promising singer—she should promise to stop singing.

## Stage

- He didn't stay for the second act of the play because it said on the program: "Act 2, a week later."
- He's a natural actor—he can really put the ham in Hamlet.
- The only reason he loves acting in Shakespearean plays is because he gets to wear tights.
- As Dorothy Parker once said, "Go see her perform; see her show the gamut of emotions from A to B."
- As a critic once said, "He played the King as if he feared someone was about to play the Ace."
- Her first big break was in the school Thanksgiving pageant. She was a squash. Typecasting, I guess.

# BACHELORS & BACHELORETTES

- His idea of a seven-course meal is a six-pack and a pickle.
- Hear that a woman just returned his ring? The envelope was marked "Glass—Handle with Care."
- She's smart—a regular encyclopedia. One thing she doesn't know—reference books are never taken out.
- Some might think that [name] is pretty smart to have stayed single all

these years. I think Ed Wynn summed it up best when he said a bachelor is a "man who never makes the same mistake once."

- Helen Rowland said it best about married men and single men. And I quote, "Never trust a husband too far nor a bachelor too near."

- He enjoys being a bachelor. Why? The only reason I can come up with is best expressed in a quote by Helen Rowland. She says, "A bachelor never quite gets over the idea that he is a thing of beauty and a boy forever."

- He's a bachelor and I hate bachelors. Why? I feel they're good-for-nothing assholes who cheat deserving women out of their divorce settlements.

- She believes in life, liberty, and the happiness of pursuit.

- He's always footloose and fiancée free.

- The only months in which she'd consider getting married are those with a "q" in them.

- She's not beyond being bowled over by a handsome guy. Just the other day she met someone and right away she was a different woman—she gave a fake name and phone number.

- He's a bachelor of arts, because he has the art of staying a bachelor.

- He's quite the lady's man. In fact, women are amazed at how well he dresses and how quickly too.

- Hey, nobody can accuse the woman of being thoughtless. Many times she's thought about taking a husband. Her only problem is whose husband to take.

- Her parents used to give her so much grief about settling down and getting married, she'd pray to the heavens for God to send them a son-in-law so they'd get off her back.

- His last girlfriend is wondering who's kissing him now—and why.

- She goes to the movies alone. Unfortunately, she has to change her seat three or four times before someone finally annoys her.

- He was two-thirds married once. He was there, the minister was there, but the bride had forgotten to show up.

- I heard at one point she had a slight disagreement with her fiancé. It seemed she wanted a big church wedding, and he didn't want to get married.

- He's such a romantic. One time he asked a girlfriend if she'd say those three little words that would make him the happiest man in the world. So she said, "Go drown yourself."

# BASTARDS

- He has a great sense of humor. He thinks, as Will Rogers once said, that "Everything is funny as long as it is happening to someone else."

- Errol Flynn had the same problem he has. Here's how Flynn described it: "My problem lies in reconciling my gross habits with my net income."

- Give him enough rope and he'll hang you.

- If he had his conscience taken out, it would be a minor operation.

- He's a man of convictions—and he has served time for every one.

- He has a surefire way of handling temptation—he yields to it.

- He has a lot in common with Ernest Hemingway. In describing Hemingway, Dorothy Parker once said, "Ernest didn't want to be nice. He just wanted to be worshipped."

- He thinks of his co-workers as family—he's always referring to them as "mothers."

- His competitive spirit and dubious sense of fair play remind me of Margot Asquith's quip that David Lloyd George "could never see a belt without hitting below it."

- He's as generous as a banker, or as Robert Frost once said, "He'll

29

lend you an umbrella in fair weather and ask for it back when it begins to rain."

- He treats all players the same—like dogs.

- He's not such a bad guy. He's like Jack Warner, about whom Simone Signoret said, "He bore no grudge against those he had wronged."

- His philosophy of forgiveness comes from the great German poet and genius Heinrich Heine who wrote, "One should forgive one's enemies, but not before they are hanged."

- His idea of free speech is using someone else's phone.

- He made a significant donation to an old-age home: He gave them his parents.

- He has all of the integrity of Richard Nixon.

- He believes the immortal advice of Jerome K. Jerome who wrote that "It is always the best policy to speak the truth, unless of course, you are an exceptionally good liar." And our guest tonight is exceptionally good.

- He carries fire insurance not life insurance because he's pretty confident where he's going to end up.

- He wants you to believe that he's really politically aware, but the truth is, the only reason he hires the handicapped is because he thinks they're fun to watch.

- If he could, he'd invent a morning-after pill for men. You know how it'd work? It would change your blood type.

- He's a man of principles, and like Harpo Marx's observations of Oscar Levant, "He never sponged off anybody he didn't admire."

- In his will, he's leaving nothing to his wife. Why? Because he wants at least one person to feel sorry he died.

- He smiles a lot—but that doesn't mean he's friendly. Remember Arthur Bloch's observation that "The man who can smile when things go wrong has thought of someone he can blame it on."

- He's a helpful kind of guy, or as F. Scott Fitzgerald once said of Ernest Hemingway, he's "always willing to lend a helping hand to one above him."

- There are many things you could say about him. That he's modest, kind, bright, and polite. They'd all be lies; but you could say them.

- As Gilbert of Gilbert and Sullivan once said, "No one can have a higher opinion of him than I have; and I think he is a dirty little beast."

- In my book, he's a great guy; but my book is fiction.

- Sharks give him professional courtesy.

# BIRTHDAYS

- You can't question a person who says he's only twenty-nine years old. Somebody who sticks to the same story for five years must be telling the truth.

- If he puts the right number of candles on his birthday cake, it would be a fire hazard.

- She had enough candles on her last birthday cake to give everyone there a suntan.

- The guests tried to count the candles on her cake, but the heat drove them back.

- As you've probably noticed, the candles on his cake are not a true representation of the birthday boy's age. We tried to put the exact number of candles on the cake, but by the time we had lit the last one, the first ones were a puddle of wax.

- He's the only man I know who, when asked what he was getting for his wife on her birthday, answered, "Make me an offer."

- Sometimes I question the true age of our guest of honor. I wouldn't be surprised if she followed a practice Oscar Wilde commented on.

He said, "Thirty-five is a very attractive age. London society is full of women of the very highest birth who have, of their own free choice, remained thirty-five for years."

- Bob Hope was most diplomatic when discussing the white lies many of us tell about how old we are. I think he had our guest of honor in mind when he remarked, "She said she was approaching forty, and I couldn't help wondering from what direction."

# BITCHES

- She's the quintessential divorce lawyer. To drum up business, she sends out fifteen hundred perfumed valentines signed, "Guess who?"

- I've finally figured out why she is never attacked by sharks. Professional courtesy.

- The only person she's jealous of is Dorothy Parker. Parker was the woman with the poisoned tongue who said, "If all the girls attending the Yale prom were laid end to end, I wouldn't be surprised."

- She's a real trooper. You know what her definition of natural childbirth is? Absolutely no makeup.

- This woman gives a whole new definition to sex kitten. You know what I've heard she likes to say just before she climaxes? "Sorry, Mom, I've got to hang up now. . . ."

- I don't have any big complaints about her. It's just that she makes me feel like Rodney Dangerfield. He complains that "My wife wants her sex in the back seat of a car—but she wants me to drive."

- What's the difference between her and a pit bull? Why the jewelry, of course.

- The only difference between her and a terrorist is that the terrorist makes fewer demands.

- I don't want to sound too harsh but, as Rex Reed once said about Barbra Streisand, "To know her is not necessarily to love her."

- Her idea of perfect sex is simultaneous headaches.

- When I heard that she did it doggie style, I was amazed. I hadn't realized she was so progressive. Then I found out what her definition of doggie style is; he gets on all fours and begs while she rolls over and plays dead.

- She's a superb strategist when it comes to relationships and very much like Zsa Zsa Gabor who once bragged, "I'm a wonderful housekeeper. Every time I get a divorce, I keep the house."

- She is even forgiving of her former lovers. She's like Zsa Zsa Gabor who said, "I never hated a man enough to give him his diamonds back."

- The only time she ever has a heart is when she's playing cards.

- She's very much like the gossip columnist Hedda Hopper about whom Casey Shawhan said, "Timid? As timid as a buzzsaw."

- She graduated from the Joan Rivers Charm School.

- C. S. Lewis knew a woman like her. He once said, "She's the sort of woman who lives for others—you can tell the others by their hunted expressions."

- She's a strong woman. Okay, maybe an intimidating woman. In fact, when I think of her, I'm reminded of something George Shultz once said about Margaret Thatcher: "If I were married to her, I'd be sure to have dinner ready when she got home."

- What do you call it when she makes love with her partner? Competition.

- Having women in the office was supposed to make us nicer, less competitive people. It didn't turn out that way. Our guest of honor and her fellow women are tigers. It's just as H. L. Mencken said, "When women kiss it always reminds me of prize fighters shaking hands."

- Her motto is, To err is human, but blame the other guy when you do.

- Her idea of open-mindedness is dating a Canadian.

- The only difference between her and a barracuda is the nail polish.

- She's as subtle as a tank.

# BORES & BOREDOM

- He talks twice as fast as anyone can listen.

- She brightens up a room when she leaves.

- The sharpness of his tongue is only exceeded by the dullness of his mind.

- Only her red, bloodshot eyes keep her from being entirely colorless.

- She had a charisma bypass.

- He's the only golfer who falls asleep during his own backswing.

- You can have some lovely moments with him, but it's like listening to Wagner. As Rossini said, "Monsieur Wagner has lovely moments but some terrible quarters of an hour."

- As someone once said about Kaiser Wilhelm II of Germany, "He can be most fascinating and wins hearts wherever he goes—and doesn't stay."

- She's a bore. And do you know what a bore is? Well, Ambrose Bierce said it best when he defined a bore as "A person who talks when you wish him to listen."

- Whenever I find myself talking with her, I'm reminded of a Hedda Hopper quote. She said, "For the first time in my life, I envied my feet. They were asleep."

- Some people say he has a bad personality. That's not really so. He has no personality at all.

- She is the most reliable, consistent woman I have ever met. Which brings to mind Bernard Berenson's comment that "Consistency requires that you be as ignorant today as you were a year ago."

- Her life is so slow, she actually looks forward to dental appointments.

- His work may not be exciting, but it serves a purpose. As Oscar Levant said about Steve Allen's writing, "When I can't sleep, I read a book by Steve Allen."

- Some people say he's lost his edge. Not so. As Chevy Chase said about Bob Hope, "Bob Hope is as funny as he ever was. I just never thought Bob Hope was that funny in the first place."

- She's so boring, she can't even entertain a doubt.

- It's true, he's a man of few words. The trouble is, he keeps repeating them.

- She has always been an unbearable bore. In fact, when she was seven, her parents ran away from home.

- Only his varicose veins save him from being completely colorless.

- If you see two women together and one looks bored, she's the other.

- There's no doubt he's trying—in fact, he's very trying.

- He deprives you of privacy without providing you with company.

- She's very cultured—she can bore you on any subject.

- He's so good at making his guests feel at home; and that's where they wish they were.

- Her vocabulary is small, but the turnover is terrific.

- To the bore: May he give us a few brilliant flashes of silence.

- She's so boring that when she took a career-aptitude test, they said she should be an anesthesiologist.

- We call him history, because he always repeats himself.

- Unfortunately, she never goes without saying.

- She monotonizes every conversation.

- You watch him in action and say, "Why isn't he on TV—so I could turn him off?"

- The man is one of the more influential people I know, which brings to mind a quip by Samuel Johnson who once said, "He is not only dull himself, but the cause of dullness in others."

# BOSSES, BAD

- He follows what is called the mushroom theory of management. He keeps us in the dark and feeds us shit.

- Having her run the company is like having Stevie Wonder direct traffic.

- He loves the working man; he loves to see them work.

- When you enter her office, you have to kiss her ring. Unfortunately, she keeps the ring in her back pocket.

- He's like the famous Hollywood boss about whom F. Scott Fitzgerald said, "You always knew where you stood with Sam Goldwyn: nowhere."

- Have you read the chairman's contract? If he dies, they bury one of the vice presidents.

- People could listen to the boss for hours—they have to.

- Due to an outbreak of AIDS, it is no longer necessary to kiss the boss's ass.

- His staff is taking skiing lessons so that they can go downhill with him.

- When she became the department head, they replaced the office sign reading SMILE with a new one reading SMILE ANYWAY.

- You can't help admiring her. If you don't you're fired.

- You can't get anywhere with him by shaking his hand when he puts it out—you have to kiss it.

- She has an ideal way of ending office meetings. She says, "All opposed to my plan say, 'I resign.'"

- He's an executive with initiative. You can always count on him to get the bull rolling.

- Her father, a successful salesman, taught her everything about business. And she hasn't forgotten a word her father said. She still never gives anyone credit.

- She must believe that charity belongs in the home—because she doesn't bring any into the office.
- All of his favorite employees wear the same cologne—it smells like fear.
- We call her the earthquake geologist: She's always finding faults.
- He refers to the company accountant as "one of the little things that count."

# BUSINESS, BAD

- This company is the first nuthouse ever run by the inmates.
- Having women in the office was supposed to make us nicer, less competitive people. It didn't turn out that way. Our guest of honor and her fellow women are tigers. It's just as H. L. Mencken said, "When women kiss it always reminds me of prize fighters shaking hands."
- She's got a great head for business. In fact, if she wasn't working for us, she'd probably go into prostitution, because, as she's quick to point out, and I quote, "You got it, you sell it, you still got it."
- We're a non-profit organization. We don't mean to be, but we are.
- He's kept his job so long by keeping things so mixed up they can't fire him.

# CARS & DRIVING

- He may look mature, but he's the only guy I know who still refers to his car as a bedroom on wheels.
- She and her car have something in common—neither one fires on all cylinders.

- His car is so old he took a bumper sticker off the other day, and the bumper fell off.

- If her car was a horse, she'd have to shoot it.

- Her car is custom made—four forward gears and *five* in reverse.

- He's always out in the driveway changing the oil in his car: He'd be better off keeping the oil and changing the car.

- She's got the only car I have ever seen that has roaches.

- His car is so old, his insurance policy covers fire, theft, and Indian raids.

- He went to the James Dean driving school.

- She's the type of person you'd like to run into sometime—like when you're driving and she's walking.

- She's been stopped for speeding so many times, the state troopers have finally given her a season's ticket.

- He always does a bang-up job of driving.

- He's getting cautious in his old age—he now slows down for stoplights.

# CHARITY

- She works a lot for charity—she has to, no one's likely to pay her.

- Every year he plays Santa Claus. It makes the kids feel so happy—and he gets to feel normal—because Santa is only expected to come once a year.

- She must believe that charity belongs in the home—because she doesn't bring any into the office.

- He's charitable, but I wouldn't say he's modest. He reminds me of Reggie Jackson, about whom Catfish Hunter said, "He'd give you the shirt off of his back. Of course, he'd call a press conference to announce it."

- She's done a lot for the Jews—just by not being one.

# CHEAPSKATES

- Why is his nose so big? Air is free.

- Money means nothing to her. When you ask her for some, you get nothing.

- He isn't particular how people treat him—just so long as they do.

- She's so cheap, her idea of an enjoyable vacation is to stay home and let her mind wander.

- He's a man of rare gifts—it's rare when he gives one.

- He's so stingy, he won't even tip his hat.

- The only thing he ever gave away was a secret.

- The way she reaches for a check, she must have inspired the inventor of the slow-motion movie.

- When he pays you a compliment, he asks for a receipt.

- She's so stingy, she takes her son's glasses off when he's not looking at anything.

- Whenever a friend asks for money, his standard excuse is "Sorry, it's all tied up in currency."

- He's real generous. When his wife asks him for clothes money, he tells her to go to the best shops and pick something nice—just not to get caught.

- She always takes him to the best restaurants. Maybe someday she'll take him inside.

- Lend him money and you'll learn the difference between capital and labor. The money you lend him represents capital—getting it back represents labor.

- Hear that a woman just returned his ring? The envelope was marked "Glass—Handle with Care."

- She's so cheap, she got a great deal on some shirts and changed her name to match the monogram.

- When he takes a dollar bill out of his pocket, it takes George Washington a good fifteen minutes to get used to the light.

- His first job was as a window washer, and he's been sponging ever since.

- She holds onto a dollar so tight, the eagle screams.

- He would recycle toilet paper, if he could.

- He's so cheap, he buys reversible condoms.

- She got her parents a fifty-piece dinner set for their golden anniversary—a box of toothpicks.

- At her age, when she goes to bed, she turns out the lights to save money, not to fool around.

- He must be a fine sculptor—everyone is always talking about what a chiseler he is.

- She's so cheap, the only thing she'll share with anyone is a communicable disease.

- Cheap? Let's put it this way, he has one-way pockets.

- Her idea of free speech is using someone else's phone.

- The guy's cheap. He thought he'd save a few bucks by having Sears do his vasectomy. The operation was a success, except for one slight snag. Everytime he gets a hard-on, the garage door goes up.

- He's so cheap that if he has to take a woman out to dinner, he prays that she's anorexic.

- He's so cheap, when his wife asked him for fifty dollars to go shopping, he screamed, "Forty dollars? What are you gonna buy with thirty dollars?"

- He tries to make every dollar—and every girl—go as far as possible.
- She read the Sally Struthers ad that says sixteen dollars will support a child for a month in India, and she sent her kids there.
- He's so cheap, he walks off airplanes with a doggie bag.
- She's so cheap that she'll only pick up a check if it's made out to her.
- He believes in free love: He won't spend a dime on a date.
- It's unfair to say he mooches off everyone. He has standards. In fact, he's very much like Oscar Levant, whom Harpo Marx once described as "a man of principle. He never sponged off anybody he didn't admire."
- She's a dollar-a-year woman—that's what she spends, not what she makes.
- He's as cheap as Jack Benny—the guy who had to think about it when asked "Your money or your life?" Fred Allen said this about the venerable comedian, which could certainly apply to our guest of honor: "I don't want to say that Jack Benny is cheap, but he's got short arms and carries his money low in his pockets."
- It's appropriate that we give her a dinner; everyone does. She hasn't picked up a check in years.
- When she pats you on the back, she's trying to get you to cough up something.
- His daughter threatened to elope. He asked her to put it in writing.
- His girlfriend wanted pearls for her birthday, so he gave her some oysters and a rabbit's foot.

# CHEATERS

- Once he had to sign into a secure building and, out of habit, he wrote, "Mr. & Mrs. Smith."
- She's stayed in all the finest hotels—for an hour at a time.

- He's interested in her happiness. In fact, he's so interested, he hired a detective to find out who's responsible for it.

- When confronted by her husband for fooling around, she answered, "How dare you! I've been faithful to you hundreds of times!"

- The less you have to do with him, the less you'll be worse off.

- He's the kind of guy who walks up to a lady in a bar and says, "Are you looking for a husband? I'm one."

- What do you mean he's a cheater? He always gets his wedding ring back on before he sees his wife.

- Every time she goes out with a man, she runs into the same old problem. Either he's married or she is.

- He's one of the few men who keeps his eyes open when he kisses a women. Maybe that's because he's constantly on the lookout for his wife.

- She's a public relations woman. Her biggest job is keeping her relations from becoming public.

- She's the kind of woman you'd give your name to, but not your right name.

- His sound system is a mystery to him—he just doesn't know much about fidelity.

# COMPETITORS

- She's all for peace. She'll bury the hatchet—in your head.

- He's got more balls than a poolroom.

- The only difference between her and a terrorist is that the terrorist makes fewer demands.

- The good news is that he's constantly keeping his ear to the ground. The bad news is that all he's succeeded in doing is limiting his vision.

- Her competitive spirit and dubious sense of fair play remind me of Margot Asquith's quip that "David Lloyd George could never see a belt without hitting below it."

- The guy's such a tough competitor that in a jack-off competition, he'd finish first, third, and ninth.

- What do you call it when she makes love with her partner? Competition.

- Having women in the office was supposed to make us nicer, less competitive people. It didn't turn out that way. Our guest of honor and her fellow women are tigers. It's just as H. L. Mencken said, "When women kiss it always reminds me of prize fighters shaking hands."

- Competition brings out the beast in him. Unfortunately, that beast is a weasel.

- She's always good at letting other people have her way.

- His way of making a big impression on you is to walk all over you.

# COMPLAINERS

- Her local department store has a complaint department devoted just to her.

- He's the kind of guy who will clean his plate and then complain that "The chicken was a little dry."

- She would find fault in heaven.

- Usually, when he finishes a meal at a restaurant, the waiter comes by and asks, "Sir, was anything all right?"

- Her first job was as advertising director for Andersen windows—that's where she got into the habit of telling everyone about her *panes*.

# CON ARTISTS

- He's always sincere—whether he means it or not.

- She's got a great head for business. In fact, if she wasn't working for us, she'd probably go into prostitution, because, as she's quick to point out, and I quote, "You got it, you sell it, you still got it."

- He's so cheap, when his wife asked him for fifty dollars to go shopping, he screamed, "Forty dollars? What're you gonna buy with thirty dollars?"

- So far as men are concerned, she can take them or leave them. After she takes them, she leaves them.

- He doesn't mind whose means he lives beyond.

- She lives by the credo: Whatever is worth doing is worth asking somebody to do.

- The guy is such a con artist, if he murdered his parents, he'd ask the judge for mercy on the grounds that he's an orphan.

- She's got such balls, she'd take a taxi to bankruptcy court and then ask the driver in as another creditor.

- A woman tried to talk him into buying her a dress, and he talked her out of the one she was wearing.

- He's looking for a rich girl who's too proud to have her husband work.

- She's so shifty she tried to claim a tax exemption for her dead mother. Her excuse? She was still very much in her thoughts.

- He not only gets the women up to his place to see his etchings, he even sells a few.

- She has always heeded Mark Twain's advice that "To be good is noble, but to teach others to be good is nobler—and less trouble."

- He borrowed his motto from P. T. Barnum who said, "Every crowd has a silver lining."

- She's very much like a diplomat; both have the ability to take something and act as though they were giving it away.

- He talks on principles and acts on interest.

- She knifes you in the back and then has you arrested for carrying a concealed weapon.

- He's a contact man—all con and no tact.

# COOKING, CRUMBY

- His cooking defies gravity—his dishes are as heavy as lead, but they won't stay down.

- She's such an stranger to the kitchen, she got really upset when her husband told her he was going out to shoot craps. She'd never cooked a crap before.

- He's completely ignorant when it comes to baking. Once he attempted to make a pineapple upside-down cake and ended up getting a hernia—he tried to turn the oven over.

- She's so inept in the kitchen, she thinks cooking is a city in China.

- She's not the world's greatest cook. You know what she made last night for dinner? A reservation.

- If he lived by his wits, he'd starve.

- They don't serve ice at their house anymore—they lost the recipe.

- They named a dessert after him: crumb cake.

- Can she cook? Let's just say she thinks lettuce is the start of a proposition.

- Where there's smoke, she's there—cooking.

- He's burned so many slices of bread, their toaster has been declared a fire hazard.

- She once asked her husband what she'll get if she cooks another meal like the one the other evening, and he said, "My life insurance."

- Can he cook? Let's just say there're enough grounds in his coffee cup for a divorce.

- She's not a cook—she's an arsonist.

- He can dish it out, but he can't cook it.

- She dresses to kill, and cooks the same way.

- Not only is he a loving husband, but he's also very devout. Every evening at dinner he places a burnt offering in front of her.

- Talk about tact. Her family has never told her why they really pray before each meal.

- He turns your head with his looks and your stomach with his cooking.

- She's done great on her new diet: She only eats her own cooking.

- It takes him two hours to cook Minute Rice.

- His idea of a seven-course meal is a six-pack and a pickle.

- Becoming a baker was the only way she could end up rolling in dough.

- He thinks judo is what you use to make bagels.

# COWARDS

- He's such a coward, when war is declared anywhere in the world, he surrenders.

- His blood isn't blue or red—it's yellow.

- Just ask him if he's a man or a mouse—he'll squeak up.

- She knows exactly what to do when faced with a tough decision. In fact, the immortal Mary Pickford came closest to describing her ability to cope with adversity in a quote about the actor Douglas Fairbanks. She said, he "had always faced a situation the only way he knew how, by running away from it."

- She's passionate about our cause. It makes sense. As C. E. Montague said, "War hath no fury like a non-combatant."

- Her car is custom made—four forward gears and *five* in reverse.

# CRITICS

- He's always criticizing, but I usually don't let it get to me. I remember what one critic, Kenneth Tynan, said, "A critic is a man who knows the way, but can't drive the car." But if I am really upset, I think of Brendan Behan's comment that "Critics are like eunuchs in a harem: They know how it's done, they've seen it done every day, but they're unable to do it themselves."

# DEADBEATS

- His reputation is a little shaky: The cable company has him on daily billing.

- Every day, she's held up as an example: a very bad example.

- His checks are made out of rubber.

- She's not the greatest at paying her bills. We weren't surprised when the baby was overdue.

- He's so in debt, as John Barrymore so eloquently expressed it, "If it isn't the sheriff, it's the finance company. I've got more attachments on me than a vacuum cleaner."

- The easiest thing she ever ran into was debt.

- He likes a woman in good shape—more specifically, a woman who's fiscally fit.

- There was a blessed event at her friend's house: She left.

# DEVIOUS

- It's always good to see her. It means that she's not behind your back.

- No one has ever questioned his integrity—in fact, no one has ever mentioned it.

- Give her enough rope and she'll hang you.

- She has the integrity of a true politician. Funny, looking at her now, I'm reminded of J.F.K.'s comment about Barry Goldwater when he said, "Barry Goldwater is standing on his record—that's so no one can see it."

- He's a typical tricky Englishman. As someone once said, "I know why the sun never sets on the British Empire: God wouldn't trust an Englishman in the dark."

# DIET

- She's religious about dieting—the only place she doesn't eat is in church.

- He has lots of fiber in his diet, and in his head.

- She cheated on her diet, but she gained in the end.

- Give him an inch, and the whole family will be on a diet.

- She's always fighting the battle of the bulge.

- He's a constant dieter—the king of wishful shrinking.

- She's on the see food diet. She eats any food that she sees.

- He makes her so nervous, she's losing weight, but she won't leave him. Well, not until she's down to 105 pounds.

- Once she asked her daughter what she plans to do when she's as big as her mother. Her daughter answered, "Diet."

- He's a light eater. As soon as it's light, he starts to eat.

- She recently went on a fourteen-day diet, but all she lost was two weeks.

- He has no trouble at all watching his waistline—it's right there in front where he can see it.

- She was recently on a strict diet, but all she lost was her temper.

- His wife got rid of 205 pounds of ugly fat—she divorced him.

- People say he has no self-control when it comes to eating, but that's not true. There're at least two things he won't eat for dinner, and that's breakfast and lunch.

- To the king of mind over platter.

- If she were a building, she'd be condemned.

# DIVORCE

- His wife got rid of 205 pounds of ugly fat—she divorced him.

- For years he's been suffering from a pain in the neck, so he's finally getting a divorce.

- I ran into her ex-husband. He says the divorce was really expensive—but worth it.

- For their fifth anniversary, she gave him a set of luggage—packed.

- Their relationship was a collection of quests; their courtship was a quest, their marriage a conquest, and the divorce was an inquest.

- She's a superb strategist when it comes to relationships and very much like Zsa Zsa Gabor, who once bragged, "I'm a wonderful housekeeper. Every time I get a divorce, I keep the house."

- The divorce was long and drawn out until they finally came to financial terms—hers.

- Their marriage was a declaration of war, their divorce was; a declaration of peace; and the alimony, taxation without representation.

- The poor guy. He took her for better or worse and she just took him for everything.

# DRINKERS

- "What does this man have in common with a houseplant?" you ask. That's simple, they both die if they're not potted.

- She's a real class act. Last week she got into a cab and asked the driver if there was room in front for a pizza and a six-pack. "Sure," said the driver obligingly. So what did she do? She opened the partition, leaned forward, and threw up.

- The guy is a lush, but you have to give him credit for being quick on his feet. One time his wife caught him hanging out at the local bar and demanded to know what he was doing. Without stating the obvious, he whispered in a slurred voice, "Shhh. I'm working for the CIA and my assignment is to get as many White Russians to defect as I can."

- She's going to quit drinking. It hasn't affected her health yet, but she can see the writing on the floor.

- He'll never be much of a musician—he never gets past the first two bars.

- She could afford to heed the advice from that great social pundit, Ann Landers, who once said, "People who drink to drown their sorrow should be told that sorrow knows how to swim."

- He's suffering from bottle fatigue.

- She's like the great wall of China: impressively stoned.

- He thinks like Oscar Wilde who said, "Work is the curse of the drinking classes."

- She isn't drinking anymore—she isn't drinking any less, either.

- He's never hung over—he always stays drunk.

- She thinks that August is a great vintage.

- He likes to ply his dates with champagne: He calls it the wine of least resistance.

- She was on her way to becoming a real connoisseur when she cut her hand on a screw-off top.

- She's a compulsive proofreader . . . and if it's not at least eighty proof, she's not interested in it.

- We call him the jailer, because he spends so much time in front of bars.

- She got drunk once and made a pass at me. She asked me to "screw her brains out." I told her it was too late for that.

- He's not one to do things in halves—he does them in fifths.

- She's the only woman I know who was expelled from Alcoholics Anonymous. She wasn't anonymous enough to suit them.

- He goes to so many bars, his suits aren't dry cleaned—they're distilled.

- Hey, give the woman a break. She's the first to admit it only takes one drink to get her drunk. The only problem is she's not sure whether it's the sixth or seventh.

- When he donates blood, there's so much alcohol in it, the Red Cross uses it to sterilize the instruments.

- He can play a much better round of golf now. He can go around in a little less than a quart.

- If it wasn't for the olives in the martini, she'd starve to death.

- He thinks Beethoven's Fifth is a bottle.

- The Red Cross rejected her blood donation—her plasma had an olive in it.

- When pink elephants get drunk, they see him.

- Her drinking has a wide range: jocose, morose, bellicose, lachrymose, and comatose.

- If a mosquito bit him, it would die of alcohol poisoning.

- She makes a drink called the Factory Whistle—one blast and you're through for the day.

- He's a dedicated carpenter—always getting hammered.

- Last New Year's, he made a solemn resolution to cut down on wine and women. It was the most miserable three hours of his life.

# DRUGS

- He can't remember whether or not pot affects his memory.

- I called her a dope, and she took it as a compliment.

- He claims he doesn't like to do cocaine—he just likes the smell of it.

- She has unusual luggage. She's the only person I know whose pill case has wheels.

- He's so dumb that during his drug-experimenting days in college, he snorted NutraSweet thinking it was Diet Coke.

- She must have the sturdiest models on the block; she uses six tubes of glue for every model.

- I'm not saying he's a coke dealer, but he's always putting his business into other people's noses.

# ECOLOGY NUTS

- She's such a dedicated recycler—it's no wonder her husband was married to someone before her.

- He would recycle toilet paper, if he could.

- She talks for hours about acid rain—if only she'd do something about her acid breath.

- Here's one guy who's always down in the dumps.

# EGGHEADS

- The guy is extremely knowledgeable—he can bore an audience on any subject.

- She's a genius. And borrowing a quote from that famous raconteur Joey Adams, "A genius is one who can do anything except make a living."

- He's an expert at making deep rumblings from his stomach sound like deep thoughts from his brain.

- She's smart—a regular encyclopedia. One thing she doesn't know—reference books are never taken out.

- He's called a big thinker—by people who lisp.

- We're talking an avid reader here. She keeps three books by the bed: One for when she's trying to get to sleep, one for when she wakes up and can't sleep, and one for spare moments during sex.

- He has a B.A., an M.A., and a Ph.D., but no J.O.B.

- She was the kind of kid who asked for homework in sex-education class.

- He's so literal, he thinks a briefcase is where you keep your underwear.

# EGOTISTS

- You'd make a fortune if you could buy her for what you think of her and sell her for what she thinks of herself.

- He's modest, but, as Winston Churchill once said about Clement Atlee, "He has much to be modest about."

- On her last birthday, she sent her parents a telegram of congratulations.

- He's so egotistical, he's programmed his computer to applaud.

- The hardest secret she'll ever have to keep is her opinion of herself.

- The good news is that he's never had an unkind word for anyone. The bad news is that's because he's always talking about himself.

- Her vanity is in inverse ratio to her talent.

- He's so conceited, he has his X-rays retouched.

- Every time she looks in a mirror, she takes a bow.

- You could make a fortune renting his head out as a balloon.

- It's a wonder how such a big head holds such a little mind.

- You can't help admiring him. If you don't, you're fired.

- Her swelled head is just nature's wacky way to fill a vacuum.

- He's so egotistical, when he hears thunder, he takes a bow.

- You can tell she's a big wheel—she's always going around in circles.

- She's always been faithful to the one great love of her life: herself.

- He denies that he's conceited—that would mean he wasn't perfect.

- She has an endless capacity to love herself.

- He fears no competitor. Because, as Ben Franklin said, "He that falls in love with himself will have no rivals."

- You've got to say one thing for the girl: What she lacks in modesty, she makes up for in conceit.

- You know what he said to me after I accused him of being affected? "Who? *Moi?*"

- For all of those who have heard his claims of having a hard childhood and being a self-made man, remember Harold Macmillan's classic comment about Harold Wilson, "If Harold Wilson ever went to school without any boots, it was merely because he was too big for them."

- She thinks that she's the fourth person in the trinity.

- As John Bright said about Benjamin Disraeli, "He is a self-made man and worships his creator."

- As Joe Namath said about Howard Cosell, "He's the kind of guy who, when he meets someone, says very loudly, 'This must be a great day for you—meeting me.'"

- He has a lot in common with Ernest Hemingway. In describing Hemingway, Dorothy Parker once said, "Ernest didn't want to be nice. He just wanted to be worshipped."

- As Catfish Hunter said of Reggie Jackson, "He'd give you the shirt off of his back. Of course, he'd call a press conference to announce it."

- When I told her we were going to roast her, she said, "Naturally, they only crucify the innocent."

- He'd love to be in the movies. Not because he wants to act, but because, as Will Rogers noted, "The movies are the only business where you can go out in front and applaud yourself."

- He's the kind of guy who's got such a big ego, he tries to tell God what to do. His last words will probably be something like Heinrich Heine's who said, "God will forgive me: that's His trade."

- He's got a big ego, but I still like him. My feelings toward him are like Jack Paar's feelings toward Steve Allen. He said, "I'm fond of Steve Allen, but not as much as he is."

- When you enter her office, you have to kiss her ring. Unfortunately, she keeps the ring in her back pocket.

- One day he got stuck between floors with a gorgeous woman, who said, "I am a big fan of yours and I'd like to give you a blowjob." He looked at her skeptically and replied, "Yeah—what's in it for me?"

- She joined the navy so the world could see her.

- You can't win with him. I gave him grief about his ego, and he replied by quoting the musician Hector Berlioz who said, "At least I have the modesty to admit that lack of modesty is one of my failings."

- I ask you the same question that Oscar Levant once asked George Gershwin: "If you had to do it all over, would you fall in love with yourself again?"

- She gave up television—she found it took her mind off herself.

# EXHIBITIONISTS

- He went to a costume party in the nudist camp—he wore rollerskates and said he was a pull toy.

- She couldn't figure out how to handle Halloween in the nudist colony. Finally, she decided that she had enough visible varicose veins to go as a road map.

- I heard he was arrested the other day for indecent exposure. Luckily, he got off on a technicality, lack of evidence.

- The way she wears clothes, she can't even hide her embarrassment.

- Don't judge her by her clothes—there isn't enough evidence.

- The way she dresses, it's hard to tell whether she's trying to catch a man or a cold.

- Her slacks are so tight, you can tell if a coin in her pocket is heads or tails.

- If she wore her neckline any lower, you'd see her belly button.

# FAMILY

- His children filled a paternity suit.

- She's the perfect mother—always making allowances.

- Give her an inch, and the whole family will be on a diet.

- You know why he refused to have more than four children? He heard that every fifth child born in the world is Chinese.

- I wouldn't call him dumb, but immediately after his wife gave birth to their son, he asked the doctor not to tell her—he wanted to surprise her.

- Her family is very protective of her . . . they don't let her out on garbage-collection day.

- Her parents used to give her so much grief about settling down and getting married, she'd pray to the heavens for God to send them a son-in-law so they'd get off her back.

- He did a spanking good job as a father.

- He got his parents a fifty-piece dinner set for their golden anniversary—a box of toothpicks.

- Her parents never struck her, except in self-defense.

- When his daughter came up to him on the night before her wedding and announced how badly she felt leaving her mother, he said gleefully, "That's okay, sweetheart. Why don't you take her with you?"

- Her folks didn't know the meaning of *quit* until she was born.

- On his last birthday, he sent his parents a telegram of congratulations.

- As Noel Coward once said about Clifton Webb, "It must be very tough to be orphaned at seventy-one."

- We have to go back to his childhood to understand how he turned out this way. The same thing happened with Andy Kaufman. As Jerry Lawler commented, "I think that when Andy was born, his father wanted a boy, his mother wanted a girl, and they were both satisfied."

- From what I understand, she was a war baby. Her parents took one look at her and started fighting.

- As a child, he was so ugly, his parents didn't know which end to diaper.

- Her mother used to rock her to sleep—with real rocks.

- His mother said he was a treasure, and his father said, "Let's bury it."

- When she was a child, her parents almost lost her. Unfortunately, they hadn't taken her far enough into the woods.

- He makes you wish birth control could be made retroactive.

- When she was born, they celebrated with a twenty-one gun salute. Unfortunately, they missed.

- His parents were disappointed: They had wanted a child.

- I won't say what her parents think of her . . . but she's an only child.

- He made his father a millionaire—of course, his father used to be a multimillionaire.

- She's a perfect example why people should not conceive too close to a microwave.

# FASHION VICTIMS

- She's *Vogue* on the outside and vague on the inside.
- She brought her cosmetics to a make-up exam.
- She's worn that dress for so long, it's been in style seven times.
- She's a regular clotheshorse. When she puts on her clothes, she looks like a horse.
- She's not just dressed—she's upholstered.
- She wears clinging dresses. She's been clinging on to the one she's wearing for years.
- That's a nice dress she's wearing. Her friends wonder if the style will ever come back.
- If she wore her neckline any lower, you'd see her belly button.
- Her hat looks as if it had made a forced landing on her head.
- What's red, green, blue, yellow, purple, and orange? [Name] all dressed up.
- She's living proof of Heinrich Heine's observation about women. He noted that "As soon as Eve ate the apple of wisdom, she reached for the fig leaf; when a woman begins to think, her first thought is of a new dress."
- She's a little neurotic about fashion. She's like Nancy Reagan, about whom Joey Adams said, "Nancy has this recurring nightmare—she's kidnapped, taken to A&S, and forced to buy dresses right off the rack."
- He couldn't pass the dress code at Kmart.
- He dresses to kill, and cooks the same way.

# FRIENDS, FALSE

- I want credit for defending my friend's honor. Yesterday, someone said that she wasn't fit to eat with pigs, and I countered, "She certainly is!"

58

- He's a true friend. Like John Barrymore, whose last words to his friend Gene Fowler were "Tell me, Gene, is it true that you are the illegitimate son of Buffalo Bill?"

- He thinks women have their own language. Since I'm his best female friend, he once asked me what the word *Isitinyet* means.

- She's a true friend. I can call her at any hour of the night and pour my heart out and be sure that she won't remember a thing in the morning.

- He's a real fair-weather friend. As Robert Frost said about a banker, "He'll lend you an umbrella in fair weather and ask for it back when it begins to rain."

- I want you all to know I defended this man the other day. Someone called him a bucket of shit and I immediately shot back, "Hey! He's no bucket!"

- He's one of those men who can't take a joke—like Winston Churchill. George Bernard Shaw once sent a telegram to Churchill that said, AM RESERVING TWO TICKETS FOR YOU FOR MY PREMIERE. COME AND BRING A FRIEND—IF YOU HAVE ONE. Churchill wired back, IMPOSSIBLE TO BE PRESENT FOR THE FIRST PERFORMANCE. WILL ATTEND THE SECOND—IF THERE IS ONE.

# GAMBLING

- She knows from experience that the best way to make a small fortune is to go to a casino with a big fortune.

- He's not much of a gambler—yesterday he asked me which was better: a full house or five aces.

- She's yet to learn that, as Wilson Mizner once said, gambling is "the sure way of getting nothing for something."

- He was setting up a race for three year olds. Some parents will do anything.

- She thinks that 9 to 5 is a reasonable set of odds.

- He's so dumb, he thinks the Kentucky Derby is a hat.

- He claims his furniture goes back to Louis the fourteenth. It will, if he doesn't pay Louis on the thirteenth.

- She claims she has enough money to live for the rest of her life, and she has, too—if she dies next week.

- He'll bet anyone 5 to 1 that he can quit gambling.

- She's such a stranger to the kitchen, she got really upset when her husband told her he was going out to shoot craps. She'd never cooked a crap before.

# GOLDDIGGERS

- I understand her latest boyfriend has a real gift for lovemaking—usually it's a pearl necklace.

- She started young—her first words were "Hey sailor."

- Her resume has one sentence on it: It says, "I swallow."

- Ask her if she's free to go out on a date, and she answers, "No, but I'm reasonable."

- All those jewels do a lot for her, but then, she does a lot for them.

- She struggled for years to get that diamond necklace. Then she stopped struggling and got it.

- She said she'd do almost anything for a fur coat, and when she got it she couldn't button it.

- She's no fool. She usually wears a perfume that brings out the mink in the man without stirring up the wolf.

- She's a good listener—when money talks.

- She likes a man whose conversation sparkles—with things like diamonds, emeralds, rubies, and pearls.

- She doesn't mind guys who love her and leave her, provided they leave her enough.

- She denies that she married him because he inherited a fortune from his father. She maintains she would have married him no matter who left him the fortune.

- When she runs her hands through a man's hair, little does he realize it's his scalp she's after.

- Her idea of a romantic setting is one that has a diamond in it.

- Don't tell anybody, but I understand she uses a gold diaphragm because she likes it when her lovers come into money.

- You know what her favorite sexual position is? Facing Bloomingdale's.

- She's a superb strategist when it comes to relationships and very much like Zsa Zsa Gabor who once bragged, "I'm a wonderful housekeeper. Every time I get a divorce, I keep the house."

- She is even forgiving of her former lovers. She's like Zsa Zsa Gabor who said, "I never hated a man enough to give him his diamonds back."

- She wants her men to make all of their advances in cash.

- She's got a million-dollar smile. She only smiles at people who have a million dollars.

- She's proof of Samuel Butler's statement that "Brigands demand your money or your life; women require both."

- She likes a man in good shape—more specifically, a man who's fiscally fit.

- She thinks any woman who goes to a male psychologist should have her head examined. Why should she lie down on a man's couch, and then pay him?

- Her morals are a little loose. She once borrowed one hundred dollars from me, saying she'd pay it back as soon as she could get back on her back.

# GOSSIPS

- The sharpness of his tongue is only exceeded by the dullness of his mind.

- And we should appreciate what a miracle her tongue is. As Washington Irving said, "A sharp tongue is the only edged tool that grows keener with constant use."

- She's as sweet and gentle as Rona Barrett, the woman Johnny Carson was talking about when he said, "She doesn't need a steak knife. Rona cuts her food with her tongue."

- She may be a miss, but she doesn't miss much.

- He picks up more dirt on the telephone than he ever could with a vacuum cleaner.

- He suffers from acute indiscretion.

- She leads a double life—hers and his.

# HOBBIES

## Cards

- She says playing cards may not be real sexy, but at least she gets to do some hand holding.

- He's not much of a gambler—yesterday he asked me which was better: a full house or five aces.

- She's not much of a card player. When we started talking about suits, she wanted to know why we were going to get dressed up.

- He's not much of a card player. He thinks shuffling is walking while dragging your feet.

## Checkers/Chess

• He had to take steroids to be on the chess team.

• She's so far out of shape that checkers is an aerobic sport.

• He's so out of shape, he gets winded playing chess.

• She prefers the odds in chess to those she found in dating; for every game of chess results in a mating.

## Climbing

• He admits that his hobby is repelling, but he still does it.

• The only climbing she ever does is social climbing.

## Coin Collecting

• I've never met anyone with more excuses for holding on to their coins.

• The only reason he took up coin collecting is because someone mentioned something about good-looking heads and tails.

• She likes to be referred to as a coin collector—when she's really just a penny-pincher.

## Dancing

• They told me she could really cut a rug—turned out she installs carpets.

• He's light on his feet—and in his head.

• She does an enthusiastic polka—no matter what the band is playing.

• As a square dancer, he missed his calling.

- He's always on his toes—and everyone else's.
- Watching the toe dancers at the ballet, she wanted to know why they didn't get taller women.
- The way she dances, it looks like a vertical expression of a horizontal idea.
- Watching him dance, I'm reminded of a Sally Poplin quote, "He makes you feel more danced against than with."

## Gardening

- The only thing he grows in his garden is tired.
- She's so polite at work—but like her flowers, she grows wild in the woods.
- He's always out on a limb.
- She has a green thumb. She can't garden worth a damn, but her thumb *is* green.

## Insect Collecting

- She had an extensive insect collection, until the cleaning lady came.
- You know what he and a pile of manure have in common? They're both insect collectors.

## Jigsaw Puzzles

- Once she discovered jigsaw puzzles, her whole world went to pieces.
- He likes jigsaw puzzles. It's the only way he ever gets a piece.

## Model Building

- He must have the sturdiest models on the block; he uses six tubes of glue for every model.

- She's always reading about which part fits which other part. I'm not talking about the models she puts together; I'm talking about sex manuals.

## Photography

- Of course he's a photographer—as Gore Vidal once said, "Photography is the art form of the untalented."

- She's a natural photographer—she always has a negative attitude.

- He calls himself a photographer, especially when he's on a date. Why? Because he loves to turn off the lights and see what develops.

## Sewing

- The suit she made me was almost perfect—except the trousers were a little tight around the armpits.

- I won't say that his sewing projects are funny, but he keeps his family in stitches.

- She's a natural seamstress—always needling other people.

## Shooting

- He's a natural marksman—a real son of a gun.

- She wasn't much of a marksman until she started thinking of the target as her mother-in-law.

## Stamp Collecting

- He has one of the rare seventy-dollar Xavier Hollander stamps—one dollar for the stamp and sixty-nine dollars if you want to lick it.
- It figures he's a stamp collector. Not everyone can be talked into paying more for a used stamp than for a new one.
- She's such a fanatic stamp collector, she gets upset when she has to use one to mail a letter.

## Travel

- Either she loves to travel or she's avoiding a lot of people.
- He's so used to traveling, his wife puts a paper band on the toilets at his house so he'll feel at home.

# HOME & HOVEL

- Her apartment is so small that the mice are hunchbacks.
- His house is so small that if you put the key too far in the keyhole, you break the window.
- She's comfortable on a racquetball court—she should be, it's bigger than her apartment.
- His house has a quaint cabana out back—the outhouse.
- I wouldn't say she was stupid or anything, but in order to keep her from hurting herself while working around the house, her husband had the word STOP stencilled on the top rung of the ladder.

# HOMETOWNS

- He's from ———, where, instead of ten commandments, they have six suggestions and two affirmations.
- She comes from ———, where they had to put Astroturf into the

stadium to keep the cheerleaders from grazing at halftime.

- He comes from ———, where the men are men and the sheep are nervous.

- She comes from the ———, where the old values are still important. At her grade school, for example, you had to raise your hand before you hit the teacher.

- He comes from ———, where the jewelers rent wedding rings.

- She comes from cattle country, where they teach 'em how to throw bull at an early age.

- He's so proud to come from New Jersey. You know what the best thing to come out of New Jersey is? Route 80.

- You know how the big cities have professional call girls? In our little town, we had to make do with volunteers.

- She may be the greatest woman ever to come from her block.

- He comes from a tough neighborhood. You could walk five blocks and never leave the scene of the crime.

- She comes from ———, the asshole of the country.

- You wonder why he moved here? Well, he was so famous in his home town that they gave him the keys out of the city.

- It's so rainy in ———, they call it America's kidney.

- He comes from ———, the armpit of the country.

- She's from California. Now, California isn't for everyone. As Fred Allen said, "California is a fine place to live—if you happen to be an orange."

- He's from Canada. Big deal. As Al Capone said, "I don't even know what street Canada is on."

- He's your typical closed-mouth Brit. As Heinrich Heine said, "Silence is a conversation with an Englishman."

- He's English. And my feelings about the English are the same as

Duncan Spaeth's who said, "I know why the sun never sets on the British Empire: God wouldn't trust an Englishman in the dark."

- She's a typical Texan—and she's proud of it. I just can't understand it. I'm with General Philip Sheridan who said, "If I owned Texas and Hell, I would rent out Texas and live in Hell."

# HYPOCHONDRIACS

- Hypochondria is the only disease he doesn't think he has.
- She suffers from CRS—Can't Remember Shit.
- He won't kiss his wife unless her lipstick has penicillin in it.
- I don't know if you have the same problem I do, but sometimes when she gets a slight cold, I'm not sure whether I should call a doctor or a drama critic.
- He won't even talk on the phone to anyone who has a cold.
- We call her the beekeeper—she's always out with hives.
- He left his job because of illness and fatigue—his boss got sick and tired of him.
- She's a manic depressive—easy glum, easy glow.
- He's the only person I know who thinks Moby Dick is a social disease, asphalt is a proctological condition, and that Ping-Pong balls are a Chinese venereal disease.
- It took her surgeon an hour to perform the operation—it'll take her a month to describe it.

# IMMATURITY

- Don't ever call her immature. She'll hold her breath and throw a tantrum.
- He couldn't concentrate today. He couldn't find his Teddy bear.

- She knows exactly what to do when faced with a tough decision. In fact, the immortal Mary Pickford came closest to describing her ability to cope with adversity in a quote about the actor Douglas Fairbanks. She said, he "had always faced a situation the only way he knew how, by running away from it."

- He's like John Belushi whom Dan Ackroyd called, "A good man, but a bad boy."

- She's not so hard to take. You just need the right attitude. As Michael Joseph said, "Authors are easy enough to get on with—if you are fond of children."

- He's like Eddie Fisher, whom Rona Barrett described as "Never very bright and, emotionally speaking, he wasn't ready for his bar mitzvah at thirty."

# INSULTS

- If I knew I was going to become a crabby old person like her, I'd kill myself now.

- This is a guy who loves his dog. In fact, he loves his dog so much he married her. Why? He had to.

- You know that, after a while, people start to look like their dogs; you got to feel sorry for her dog.

- I'll never forget the first time I met her, but I'll keep trying.

- As Walter Kerr would say, "He has delusions of adequacy."

- I ask our honoree the immortal question once asked by Oscar Levant, "If you had to do it all over, would you fall in love with yourself again?"

- He may be the greatest man ever to come from his block.

- Nor do I buy her holier than thou act. I've been around for a while—I knew her when. As Grouch Marx once said, "I've been around so long, I knew Doris Day before she was a virgin."

- When they say he does the work of two men, take it with a grain of salt. Remember Joey Adams's quip about Ronald Reagan: "Reagan has done the work of two men—Laurel and Hardy."

- Sure, he keeps his ear to the ground. But as Joseph Cannon said about President William McKinley, "McKinley keeps his ear to the ground so close that he gets it full of grasshoppers much of the time."

- This woman is an unholy terror—like Hitler. And as Franklin Delano Roosevelt said about Adolf, "The world is too small to provide adequate living for both Hitler and God."

- There is less to him than meets the eye.

- As they say in Iran, "May the fleas of a thousand camels infect your armpits."

- Let us not exaggerate his faults. There is still hope—there always is. As Alexander Woollcott said about Oscar Levant, "There's nothing wrong with Oscar Levant that a miracle cannot fix."

- Elbert Hubbard said, "If you can't answer a man's arguments, all is not lost; you can still call him vile names." Good advice. Our guest is often right, but he's still a douche bag.

- Feel free to insult our guest of honor. I know that Philip Chesterfield said that "An injury is much sooner forgotten than an insult," but don't worry. This guy's memory isn't that good.

- As Russell Lynes once said, "The only graceful way to accept an insult is to ignore it; if you can't ignore it, top it; if you can't top it, laugh at it; if you can't laugh at it, it's probably deserved." And our guest has been laughing a lot tonight.

- Why should I be nice? The fool came here to be roasted, and, as Pierre Corneille said, "He who allows himself to be insulted deserves to be."

- I think of her reports the way Dorothy Parker thought of a novel when she said, "This is not a novel to be tossed aside lightly. It should be thrown with great force."

- He's your typical closed-mouth Brit. As Heinrich Heine said, "Silence is a conversation with an Englishman."

- She's English. And my feelings about the English are the same as Duncan Spaeth's who said, "I know why the sun never sets on the British Empire: God wouldn't trust an Englishman in the dark."

- New employees learn about him right away—just as new playwrights learn about Henry Arthur Jones. What the playwrights learn is Oscar Wilde's comment that "The first rule for a young playwright to follow is not to write like Henry Arthur Jones. The second and third rules are the same."

- She is the voice of experience in our office. And you know how that came about. As Pete Seeger said, "Education is when you read the fine print. Experience is what you get when you don't."

- Just looking at him, I can tell that sex with this man would probably be akin to poetry in motion. Something along the lines of: "Slam, bam, thank you ma'am."

- When you meet her, you like her. But, as you get to know her, your feelings change. Or as Alice Roosevelt Longworth once said of Thomas E. Dewey, "You really have to get to know Dewey to dislike him."

- When she goes by, I'm reminded of Bette Davis's line, "There goes the good time that was had by all."

- You know what the difference is between an asshole and a rectum? You can't put your arm around a rectum. [Use accompanying gesture.]

- I'll bet he's never had a case of hemorrhoids in his life. How do I know? Easy, he's a perfect asshole.

- She suffers from CRS—Can't Remember Shit.

# JEALOUSY

- She's so jealous, if she doesn't find any blond, red, or brunette hairs on her husband's jacket, she accuses him of having an affair with a bald woman.
- She's so jealous, she had male bridesmaids.
- He's the jealous type, but he doesn't keep track of his wife's affairs. . . . He hired a detective to do that.

# JUVENILE DELINQUENTS

- He was the kind of kid who asked for homework in sex-education class.
- She's an honor student. She's always saying, "Yes, your honor. No, your honor."
- He has no respect for age unless it's bottled.
- When she was little, she used to steal hubcaps from moving cars.

# LAZYBONES

- She thought she was getting a model husband. Unfortunately, he wasn't a working model.
- He helps clean the house too—he sits in front of the TV and gathers dust.
- He's the only member of the glazier's union who doesn't do windows.
- Her idea of exercise is jumping to conclusions.
- He's like Jerome K. Jerome who once said, "I love work—I can watch it all day."
- The only reason she gets up from bed in the morning is because she can't carry it with her during the day.
- He's such a slug, he won't even exercise discretion.

- She's too lazy to watch her figure, so the boys don't either.

- He's so lazy, when he gets a cold even his nose won't run.

- Believe it or not, she's known as a miracle worker—it's a miracle when she works.

- He's a real steady worker. If he gets any steadier, he'll be motionless.

- She's very consistent. She works eight hours and sleeps eight hours—unfortunately, they're the same eight hours.

- He's not afraid of work—he's fought it successfully for years.

- She's so lazy, if opportunity knocked, she'd complain about the noise.

- Who says nothing is impossible. She's been doing nothing for years.

- He's not afraid of hard work—in fact, he can sleep right next to it.

- She's not much of a go-getter. Let me give you a piece of advice: Remember the words of Sophie Tucker who said, "I have been poor and I have been rich. Rich is better."

- If she were an office product, she'd be stationery.

- He loves the working man; he loves to see him work.

- We want to get her something she's never had: a job.

# LIARS

- It's hard to find a polite way to comment on his imaginative interpretations of reality, so I'll quote Richard Brinsley Sheridan who said, "The right honorable gentleman is indebted to his memory for his jests and to his imagination for his facts."

- Never question her math. Everything balances. As Diane de Poitiers said, "The years that a woman subtracts from her age are not lost. They are added to the ages of other women."

- He always aims to tell the truth, but he has really bad aim.

- You need to have a great memory to be as good a liar as she is.

- He reminds me of an all-night dice game: a lot of crap.

- Her excuses are shakier than a hula dancer.

- When he puts his cards on the table, he usually has another deck up his sleeve.

- He's a second-story man—nobody believes his first story.

- She doesn't kiss and tell, she kisses and exaggerates.

- I don't know if I'd call him a liar, but one time he dislocated both shoulders describing a fish he caught.

- You can tell when she's lying—her lips are moving.

- He believes the immortal advice of Jerome K. Jerome who wrote that "It is always the best policy to speak the truth, unless of course, you are an exceptionally good liar." And our guest tonight is exceptionally good.

- She wouldn't even tell the truth in her diary.

- He majored in plagiarism.

- You can't call her a confirmed liar, because nothing she says is ever confirmed.

# LOSERS

- She plays an essential role here—like a lifeguard at a car wash.

- We're not sure what we'll do without him, but we've been dreaming about it for years.

- Having her run the company is like having Stevie Wonder direct traffic.

- He's the best argument I've ever seen for retroactive contraception.

- She started at the top and worked her way down.

- What can I compare him to? Well, the first thing that comes to mind is a Christmas tie. Both are loud and useless.

- She's the kind of person who inspired Groucho Marx to say, "I never forget a face, but in your case I'll make an exception."

- When opportunity knocked at his front door, he was out in the backyard looking for a four-leaf clover.

- He's such a romantic. One time he asked a girlfriend if she'd say those three little words that would make him the happiest man in the world. So she said, "Go drown yourself."

- Her staff is taking skiing lessons so they can go downhill with her.

- He deserves credit for everything he's done. In the words of Joseph Heller, "He was a self-made man who owed his lack of success to nobody."

- My review of her efforts would have to sound like Walter Kerr's review of a play when he said that "*Hook and Ladder* is the sort of play that gives failures a bad name."

- Give the guy a break. He really only has two faults—everything he says and everything he does.

- Everyone has the right to have some faults, but she abuses the privilege.

- He used to be pretty popular with the girls. In fact, once, two women fought a duel over him to see who'd get him. One got him in the leg and the other got him in the arm.

- She has no equals—only superiors.

- He's been turned down more often than a bed.

- There definitely was something about her that I liked. Unfortunately, she spent it.

- He's such a loser, the only way he can get a date is to tear one off a calendar.

- The guy's such a loser that once a prostitute said to him, "Not now—I have a headache."

- She's such a big nothing, she has to rent a shadow.

- I'll never forget the first time I met him, but I'll keep trying.

- She's an inspiration to us all—if she can make it, we certainly can.

- We've all watched as he sought to find himself—and all wondered how he would deal with the inevitable disappointment.

- The President has made a cabinet post for her: Secretary of the Inferior.

- He has a good grasp of his own sexuality; and that's the only sex he gets.

- As Walter Kerr said, "He has delusions of adequacy."

- His wife put a mirror over the bed—she likes to watch herself laugh.

- In college, she studied glass blowing—and she still blows every job she gets.

- He got tattoos, because it was the only way he could walk around with a girl on each arm.

- She's ugly, annoying, and dishonest—and those are her good points.

- I have one piece of advice for you—if you have your life to live over again—don't.

- He's like a coal-oil lamp: He's not especially bright, he's often turned down, he smokes, and he goes out every night.

- She once asked me if I thought she had an inferiority complex. I reassured her—I told her she was a realist.

- He once asked a girl if she could learn to love a guy like him, and she answered, "Yes, if he isn't too much like you."

- She sent her picture to the lonely-hearts club. The reply came back "We're not *that* lonely."

- The only man she ever had at her feet was a shoe salesman.

- She's such a loser, she runs into accidents that started out to happen to someone else.

- The guys such a loser, he couldn't bribe a dog to be his friend.

- She's as necessary as a fence around a cemetery.

- He's kept his job so long by keeping things so mixed up they can't fire him.

- She's as efficient as a dyslexic engraver.

- His first job was as a doorman, but he got arrested for loitering.

- Becoming a baker was the only way he could end up rolling in dough.

- She ran unopposed and lost.

- He's modest, but, as Winston Churchill once said about Clement Atlee, "He has much to be modest about."

- She followed Orson Welles's success plan. Welles said, "I started at the top and worked my way down."

- She has hidden talents; unfortunately, they're very well hidden.

- He's not the most popular of individuals. As Oscar Wilde said about W. E. Henley, "He has fought a good fight and has had to face every difficulty except popularity."

- She's been in so many self-help programs, she thinks LA stands for Losers Anonymous.

- He works a lot for charity—he has to, no one's likely to pay him.

- His boss would love to pay him what he's worth, but there's a law against paying less than minimum wage.

- She knows all the words to the *Brady Bunch* theme song. What a memory. What a geek.

# LOUDMOUTHS

- Sometimes he's thoughtless. Never speechless, just thoughtless.

- We call her Miss Parole: She never lets anyone finish a sentence.

- He can talk louder than a television commercial.

- She doesn't only engage in conversation—she syndicates it.
- Can he talk? Hell, he's been known to speak 150 words a minute, with gusts up to 200.
- She thinks she's a siren, but she only sounds like one.
- The only thing that can cheat him out of a last word is an echo.
- He has let his mind go blank, but he's forgotten to turn off the sound.
- It took her surgeon an hour to perform the operation—it'll take her a month to describe it.
- He can even talk for hours about the value of silence.
- She talks on principles and acts on interest.
- He regards free speech not as a right, but as a continuous obligation.
- She only opens her mouth to change feet.
- Their marriage is a partnership, only he's the silent partner.
- When she gets a case of laryngitis, it's like the phone has been disconnected.
- He can be outspoken—but only by someone with a megaphone.
- She never opens her mouth without subtracting from the sum of human knowledge.
- He approaches every subject with an open mouth.
- I don't know about you people, but I used to think there was no such thing as a perpetual-motion machine until I saw her mouth in motion.
- He talks twice as fast as anyone can listen.
- There's another explanation why she wears very little makeup: her lipstick. She can't keep her mouth closed long enough to put it on.
- You'd think since he's got two ears and one tongue, he'd listen twice as much as he talks, but *nooooo*.
- He can talk—and talk—and talk. As Winston Churchill once said about Ramsay MacDonald, "We know that he has, more than any

other man, the gift of compressing the largest amount of words into the smallest amount of thought."

- She has occasional flashes of silence that make her conversation perfectly delightful.

- She can be outspoken—but I've never heard anyone do it.

- I can't believe how fast the guy talks. I think Barry Goldwater expressed this phenomenon best with his quote about Hubert Humphrey. He said, "Humphrey talks so fast that listening to him is like trying to read *Playboy* magazine with your wife turning the pages."

# MARRIAGE

- One thing she's learned during her marriage is the truth of Helen Rowland's advice: "Never trust a husband too far nor a bachelor too near."

- They have a joint checking account. He puts in the money and she takes it out.

- He was quite a dude before he got married. Now he's subdued.

- She must have hated work. Look at her husband. As Helen Rowland said, "When you see what some girls marry, you realize how much they must hate to work for a living."

- Few people would guess that she is married to such a deep thinker, such a philosopher. Of course, Socrates once said, "By all means marry: If you get a good wife, you'll be happy; if you get a bad one, you'll become a philosopher."

- He's a class act. You know what he whispered in his wife's ear on their wedding night? "Where's the reset button?"

- You know what this new bride and a criminal before sentencing have in common? They both know it'll be hard, but they don't know for how long.

- Why did God create this wonderful bride for this lucky groom? Easy. Sheep can't cook.

- Seeing these lovebirds reminds me of the immortal words of Michel de Montaigne who said, "Marriage is like a cage; one sees the birds outside desperate to get in, and those inside equally desperate to get out."

- Marriage can be overrated. I agree with Burt Reynolds who said, "Marriage is about the most expensive way for the average man to get his laundry done."

- He once found his best friend in bed with his wife and said, "Look, buddy, I have to, but you?"

- Marriage has a way of changing things. Like love. In fact, Ambrose Bierce defined love as "A temporary insanity curable by marriage."

- These are a couple made in heaven. They are a perfect example of God's mercy. One could say of them the same thing that Samuel Butler said about the Carlyles, "It was very good of God to let Carlyle and Mrs. Carlyle marry one another and so make only two people miserable instead of four."

- They're inseparable; it takes several people to pull them apart.

- You never hear any words of anger from this married couple—they finally decided to soundproof their apartment.

- Their marriage is a partnership, only he's the silent partner.

- From what I've heard, it's been so long since they've made love, she's afraid if something happens to her, he won't be able to identify the body.

- After an argument, they always patch things up—his jaw, his nose, his head.

- The last time she said yes to him was when he proposed, and he's been regretting it ever since.

- Before they were married, he was an atheist who didn't believe in hell. Now, he thinks otherwise.

- A friend once asked him what he did before he was married. And he answered with a sigh and a far-away look in his eyes: "Anything I wanted."

- You can tell who wears the pants in the family when the poor guy can't even commit suicide without asking his wife's permission.

- There's only one thing that keeps him from being a happily married man—his wife.

- After all these years of marriage, his wife can't stop kicking herself for messing up at the wedding ceremony. She had meant to say, "I do" when the minister asked, "Is there anyone present who objects to this marriage?"

- The wedding ceremony should be a snap for her, as long as she doesn't say, "I did," when she's supposed to say, "I do."

- The good news is he's been given two weeks to live. The bad news is that's how long his wife is going to be away on vacation.

- One time a friend came up to him and mentioned that his wife is an angel and he responded, "Lucky stiff, mine's still alive."

- She's so jealous, if she doesn't find any blond, red, or brunette hairs on her husband's jacket, she accuses him of having an affair with a bald woman.

- She's so jealous, she had male bridesmaids.

- In his will, he's leaving nothing to his wife. Why? Because he wants at least one person to feel sorry he died.

- His wife's an angel, all right. Her head's always in the clouds, and she's constantly harping about one thing or another.

- He's such a big mouth, his wife had laryngitis for two weeks and didn't know it.

- The poor guy. He took her for better or worse and she just took him for everything.

- She was no fool. She knew she'd never need to hire any domestic help—she married it instead.

- She thought she was getting a model husband. Unfortunately, he wasn't a working model.

- From what I understand, he's adamant about only marrying a woman who can take a joke. Luckily for him, that's the only kind who would take him.

- Her husband is real generous. When she asks him for clothes money, he tells her to go to the best shops and pick something nice—just don't get caught.

- A fortuneteller predicted that her husband was going to die soon, and she asked if she'd be acquitted.

- The only thing she asks is to see her husband's name—just once—in the obituary column.

- She's his consolation, but if it wasn't for her he wouldn't need any consolation.

- He put a ring on her finger, and she put a ring through his nose.

- She always forgives him when she's in the wrong.

- On the job application where it said marital status, he wrote, "Below wife."

- Every now and then she comes to him on bended knee—like when he hides under the bed and she's tries to pull him out.

- She's instructed payroll to mail his check home and eliminate the middleman.

- He never argues with her. He might win and then he's really in trouble.

- She went to the seashore, claiming that mountain air disagrees with her. Her husband's surprised. He can't see how it would dare.

- Despite the numbers, he can't believe married men live longer than single men—he says it only seems longer.

- She's such a creature of habit, she makes her husband help the waiter with the dishes.

- He really knows his place. When he disagrees with his wife, he puts his foot down and says, "No—and that's semifinal!"

- She has the perfect definition of compromise—when he admits he's wrong, she forgives him.

- She's thoughtful all right, for Easter she gave him a rabbit punch.

- Why does he stay with her? He has a soft spot—in his head.

- The only reason she's had five children by him is so she could lose him in the crowd.

- She's the only woman I know who, when asked what she was getting for her husband on his birthday, answered, "Make me an offer."

- He makes her so nervous she's losing weight, but she won't leave him. Well, not until she's down to 105 pounds.

- It's not that she used to be heavy. It's just that when she promenaded down the aisle after the wedding ceremony, the groom had to walk behind her.

- When his daughter came up to him on the night before her wedding and announced how badly she felt leaving her mother, he said gleefully, "That's okay, sweetheart. Why don't you take her with you?"

- He's a man of conviction—after he knows what his wife thinks.

- His wife is delighted that he's here today. While he's away, she's having his cage cleaned.

- When asked how long he's been married, he responds despondently, "Every second of the day and night."

- Her mother wasn't very supportive at first either. I believe she quoted the Ann Landers's line, "You need that guy like a giraffe needs a strep throat."

- Why do married men die before their wives? They want to.

- He's interested in her happiness. In fact, he's so interested, he hired a detective to find out who's responsible for it.

- He can't understand it when his friends ask him if he cheats on his wife. Who else is he going to cheat on?

- Once he was sick in bed for a whole week, and his secretary sent a sympathy card to his wife.

- What a natural groom—he always smells like horseshit.

- The poor guy's getting old, all right. How do I know? Well, just the other day he told me that his wife had given up sex for Lent and he didn't find out till Easter.

- He comes from ————, where the jewelers rent wedding rings.

# MEANNESS

- The only time she ever has a heart is when she's playing cards.

- He's the kind of guy who would throw an anchor to a drowning man.

- She's applying for a job as a prison warden so she can put tacks on the electric chair.

- The only thing he'd share with you willingly is a communicable disease.

- She got her parents a fifty-piece dinner set for their golden anniversary—a box of toothpicks.

- He sends get-well cards to hypochondriacs.

- She's so bad, she told her kids that Santa Claus is too old to get around anymore.

- He knifes you in the back and then has you arrested for carrying a concealed weapon.

- His girlfriend wanted pearls for her birthday, so he gave her some oysters and a rabbit's foot.

- She was engaged to a guy with a wooden leg. She got mad and broke it off.

- He's so disagreeable, his own shadow won't keep him company.

- She thinks twice before she speaks, so that she can say something nastier than if she spoke right out.

- He has the disposition of an untipped waiter.

- She has a tongue that could clip a hedge.

- He's so tough that he eats sardines without opening the can.

- She's temperamental—90 percent temper and 10 percent mental.

- He has a dynamite personality—always blowing up.

# MEN CHASERS

- She chases younger men—at her age, there are no older men.

- She took the advice of Mae West who said, "It's not the men in your life that counts, it's the life in your men."

- She gets men by using her come-on sense.

- She doesn't have a diary. That's not surprising—as Tallulah Bankhead said, "It's the good girls who keep diaries; the bad girls never have the time."

- She's writing a book about her boyfriends—she's on Chapter 89.

- She starts every morning with exercise. Usually in the form of walking home.

- Her legs are like the U.S. Army—open to all able-bodied men between eighteen and thirty-five.

- She often works undercover—not that she's a policewoman or anything.

- She's had more sailors on her than most battleships.

- If you eat at her restaurant, don't ask for the specialty of the house: She's it.

- She's been picked up so many times she's starting to grow handles.

- She's the friendly type . . . the type you can have a wonderful night with even if you play your cards wrong.

- She's a capable girl—capable of anything.

- The only time she says stop is when she sends a telegram.

- She's a public relations girl. Her biggest job is keeping her relations from becoming public.

- She's been on more laps than a napkin.

- When a guy gets fresh, she counts to ten—ten thousand.

- She leads a date-to-date existence.

- She doesn't make a practice of necking—she doesn't need any.

- The way she pretends to crawl away from temptation, no one's surprised when it overtakes her.

- She'll scream at a mouse, but she'll get into a car with a wolf.

- She was pretty popular at college. Heck, she was voted girl with whom you are most likely to succeed.

- The girl loves the outdoors—hell, she doesn't do badly indoors, either.

- She and I had a heart-to-heart not long ago, and I asked her how she always had so many boys interested in her. She answered easily, "I give up."

- Her "no" is like a comma, it doesn't mean a complete stop.

- Is she a threat in the job market? Let's just say when she was filling out a job application, under the heading SEX, she put, "Frequently."

- She's a dumb girl who didn't turn a deaf ear to a blind date.

- Easy? At school she was voted the girl most likely to conceive.

- She's charging the stork with something that should be blamed on a lark.

- She's the kind of woman you'd give your name to, but not your right name.

- She's a home girl, and she doesn't care whose.

- You have to admit, she's quite the party girl. In fact, just the other day, her boyfriend conceded that she'd given him some of the best weekends of his life.

- The wedding ceremony should be a snap for her, as long as she doesn't say, "I did," when she's supposed to say, "I do."

- I think Bette Davis best summed up the attributes of our guest of honor with a line she used to describe another actress. Davis said, "She is the original good time that was had by all."

- When I look at our guest of honor, I'm immediately reminded of a Dorothy Parker quote. She said, "The girl speaks eighteen languages and can't say 'no' in any of them."

- Is she available? In the words of Saki (or H. H. Munro), "Romance at short notice was her specialty."

- Her sound system is a mystery to her—she just doesn't know much about fidelity.

- She likes a man in good shape—more specifically, a man who's fiscally fit.

- She's the one exception to the law of gravity. It's easier to pick her up than to drop her.

- Does she chase after men? Why should she? Does a mousetrap chase after mice?

- So far as men are concerned, she can take them or leave them. After she takes them, she leaves them.

- She doesn't mind whose means she lives beyond.

- That woman is so promiscuous she failed her driver's test three times, because she couldn't learn to sit up in a car.

- She has tattooed on to the top of her head, DON'T PULL MY EARS, I KNOW WHAT I'M DOING.

- She's stayed in all the best hotels—an hour at a time.

- She is, as Tallulah Bankhead once described herself, "As pure as driven slush."

- She's been seeing a psychiatrist. And she's also been seeing a bartender, an engineer, and the mailman.

# MILITARY

- She's short all right. You know what they'd call her if she were in the navy? A microwave.

- They say old soldiers fade away. Looking at good old [name] over here, it's going to take one hell of a long time before he starts disappearing.

- What do you call a marine with a sheep under one hand and a goat under the other? A bisexual.

- He's a great soldier, but he's a bit dim. In his will, he's leaving all his money to the unknown soldier's widow.

- He's a great pilot, but he'll never get a chance to test-fly something like the Stealth bomber. Why? Because he'd be too busy honking the horn, squealing the tires, and playing the radio.

- The guy's an optimist. He's the only one I know who makes out the duty roster in ink.

- He wasn't tall enough to become a marine, so they made him a submarine.

- She joined the navy so the world could see her.

- She's such a coward, when war is declared anywhere in the world, she surrenders.

- If he had been an admiral, he'd be like a great tuna, and all his men would call out, "Hail to the mighty chicken of the sea!"

- He's patriotic, all right. But as Dr. Johnson once said, "Patriotism is the last refuge of the scoundrel."

# MOTHERS-IN-LAW

- I take what my mother-in-law says with a grain of salt. I like Les Dawson's attitude. He said, "My mother-in-law thinks I'm effeminiate, not that I mind, because, beside her, I am."

- She's worst than a terrorist. At least you can negotiate with a terrorist.

- I once called her a vulture, but that's not fair—to the vultures. At least a vulture waits until you are dead to eat your heart out.

- She's very giving—always giving advice.

- My mother-in-law did not have high expectations of me. As Hubert Humphrey said, "Behind every successful man stands a surprised mother-in-law."

- Mothers-in-law are like seeds. You don't need them, but they come with the tomato.

# NEAT-FREAKS

- We call her the holy exterminator—first sight of a bug and she says, "Let us spray."

- He cleans the house thoroughly on Wednesday, so it'll be spotless when the maid comes on Thursday.

- Her husband once got out of bed in the middle of the night to take an aspirin and came back and found that the bed was made.

- He helps clean the house, too—he sits in front of the TV and gathers dust.

# NEWLYWEDS

- One time she told me that the concept of the wedding processional made her real jittery. Then she quoted an observation by Heinrich Heine, and I got a bit anxious, too. Heine said, "Music played at weddings always reminds one of the music played for soldiers before they go into battle."

- He got married so that he could have a big family. He got one—hers.

- They're still at that stage where they eat breakfast in bed and have sex on the dining-room table.

- He's a class act. You know what he whispered in his wife's ear on their wedding night? "Where's the reset button?"

- You know what this new bride and a criminal before sentencing have in common? They both know it'll be hard, but they don't know for how long.

- Why did God create this wonderful bride for this lucky groom? Easy. Sheep can't cook.

- The wedding ceremony should be a snap for her, as long as she doesn't say, "I did," when she's supposed to say, "I do."

- She's so jealous, she had male bridesmaids.

- He thought he was getting a model wife. Unfortunately, she wasn't a working model.

- From what I understand, he's adamant about only marrying a woman who can take a joke. Luckily for him, that's the only kind who would take him.

- He put a ring on her finger and she put a ring through his nose.

- It's not that she's heavy. It's just that when she promenaded down the aisle after the wedding ceremony, the groom had to walk behind her.

- When his daughter came up to him on the night before her wedding and announced how badly she felt leaving her mother, he said gleefully, "That's okay, sweetheart. Why don't you take her with you?"

- What a natural groom—he always smells like horseshit.

# OAFS

- He learned manners by emulating his idol: Mike Tyson.

- She's like Frank Harris whom Oscar Wilde said was "invited to all the great houses in England—once."

- He's a slob all right, but I wouldn't go as far as to say he's an ape. It's not really fair to apes, because an ape peels the banana before he eats it.

- She behaves like a saint—a Saint Bernard.

- People like him don't grow on trees: They swing from them.

# OBNOXIOUS

- What kind of guy is he? Well, as Joe Namath said about Howard Cosell, "He's the kind of guy who, when he meets someone, says very loudly, 'This must be a great day for you—meeting me.'"

- As Catfish Hunter said of Reggie Jackson, "He'd give you the shirt off of his back. Of course, he'd call a press conference to announce it."

- He'll be obnoxious to the end, like the death-row prisoner about to die who asks the warden for an antacid because he's about to have some gas, or the criminal James W. Rogers who, facing a firing squad, answered the traditional last-request question by saying, "Why, yes—a bullet-proof vest."

- She would make a perfect stranger.

- As Rex Reed said about Barbra Streisand, "To know her is not necessarily to love her."

- I know her so well, I haven't spoken to her in ten years.

# OLD MEN, DIRTY

- He always goes out with younger women—he believes that you're only as old as the person you are feeling.

- He's still chasing women, but he can't remember why.

- He's eighty-two years old, but he often feels like a twenty-six-year-old; not that he ever gets one.

- He has the body of an eighteen-year-old—waiting for him in his room.

- Let's not say he's a letch—but word has it he'd fuck mud.

- Frederick Pohl said that "Isaac Asimov turned into a dirty old man at the age of fifteen." But that's quite old compared to our guest of honor.

# OPTIMISTS

- He's such an optimist, he puts his shoes on when a speaker says, "Now, in conclusion . . ."

- If he fell from the fortieth floor of a building, he'd say, "So far, so good," at the twentieth floor.

- She's so positive—but that's not necessarily a sign of wisdom. As Woody Allen said about Diane Keaton, "Keaton believes in God. But she also thinks the radio works because there are tiny people inside it."

- She's so naive, when I told her a mutual friend was having an affair, she said, "That's wonderful. Who's catering it?"

- I don't know if I'd call him naive, but he still thinks that intercourse has something to do with the state highway.

- The guy's an optimist. He's the only one I know who makes out the duty roster in ink.

- She's an optimist, not a realist. As Walter Winchell said, "An optimist is a man who gets treed by a lion, but enjoys the scenery."

- He's one of those optimists not ready for the real world. Or as Joe Garagiola once described Hugh Downs, "If Hugh woke up on Christmas day and found a pile of manure under the tree, he'd wonder where they were hiding the pony."

- She always dates her checks ahead. If she should die on, say, January 15, her tombstone will probably read: SHE DIED JANUARY 15, AS OF FEBRUARY 1.

# PESSIMISTS

- He never builds castles in the air for fear they'll have mortgages on them.

- I hear sometimes she gets so depressed, she reads the obituaries to cheer herself up.

- When he was four, he found there was no Easter Bunny and he's been cynical ever since.

- She thinks twice before she speaks, so that she can say something nastier than if she spoke right out.

- She thinks that the main function of sunlight is to cast shadows.

- Give him the choice between two evils, and he'll take both.

- He's a pessimist. He carries a card in his wallet that says, IN CASE OF ACCIDENT—I'M NOT SURPRISED.

- She's such a cynic—she thinks other people are as bad as she is.

# PESTS

- As Groucho Marx once said, "I never forget a face, but in your case I'll make an exception."

- He didn't make the list of my one thousand favorite people.

- She is like the girl in the nursery rhyme with the curl in the middle of her forehead. When she is good, she's very good. And when she is bad, she's horrid.

- Is she a pest? Well, as Lionel Barrymore said about Margaret O'Brien, "If that child had been born in the middle ages, she'd have been burned as a witch."

- He brightens up a room when he leaves.

- When you meet him, you like him. But, as you get to know him, your feelings change. Or as Alice Roosevelt Longworth once said of Thomas E. Dewey, "You really have to get to know Dewey to dislike him."

- She's not such a bad person—until you get to know her.

- I named my first ulcer after her.

- What a pest. No one will mourn when he dies. Quite the contrary. William Connor said it best: "Few men by their death can have given such deep satisfaction to so many."

- At first people don't care much for him; but he grows on them—like a wart.

- She's as oppressive as Tallulah Bankhead, about whom Howard Dietz said, "A day away from Tallulah is like a month in the country."

- He's done a lot for the Jews—just by not being one.

- She's the one perfect argument for mercy killing.

- He's such a pain in the neck, the aspirin consortium is considering paying him a royalty.

- He's not one of those guys who goes around complaining about hemorrhoids—he's a perfect asshole.

- She hasn't been herself lately. . . . It's been a big improvement.

- He's always trying . . . very trying.

- She's not a hard-boiled person—she's only half-baked.

- He gave a party for all of his friends . . . both of them.

94

- She's the type of person you'd like to run into sometime—like when you're driving and she's walking.

- He's so disagreeable, his own shadow won't keep him company.

- She makes you wish birth control could be made retroactive.

- I think that he, like Richard Brinsley Sheridan, enjoys being in trouble. As John Eldon once said of Sheridan, "Every man has his element: Sheridan's is hot water." The same applies to our guest of honor.

- It was a great day when she graduated. The teachers cried for joy—they thought she'd never leave.

# POLITICS & POLITICIANS

- Most of us got out of college and entered the real world. She didn't. She went into government.

- My view of civil servants, such as our guest of honor, was best expressed by Sir Walter Walker who said, "Britain has invented a new missile. It's called the civil servant—it doesn't work and it can't be fired."

- I don't think much of politicians. I'm with H. L. Mencken who said, "A politician is an animal which can sit on a fence and yet keep both ears to the ground."

- He's an honest politician. At least, by Simon Cameron's definition. He said that "An honest politician is one who, when he is bought, will stay bought."

- She's the perfect politician, once she makes up her mind, she's full of indecision.

- He ran unopposed and lost.

- Her motto is, To err is human, but blame the other guy when you do.

- He's always sincere—whether he means it or not.

- In crime, it's take the money and run. In politics, it's run, then take the money.

- As I reviewed her political record, I was reminded of Joey Adams's comment about Ronald Reagan. He said, and I quote, "Reagan has done the work of two men—Laurel and Hardy."

- He's a real politician: He really knows his ass from his elephant.

- There are two sides to every issue—and she takes them both.

- He meets George Bernard Shaw's criteria for a politician: "He knows nothing, and he thinks he knows everything. That points clearly to a political career."

- When he told his wife he'd been elected, she exclaimed, "Honestly?" "Why do you have to change the subject?" he complained.

- She's the quintessential politician. She's very adept at repairing her fences by hedging.

- He shakes your hand before the election and your confidence after.

- She has the integrity of a true politician. Looking at her now, I'm reminded of J.F.K.'s comment about Barry Goldwater when he said, "Barry Goldwater is standing on his record—that's so no one can see it."

- He's one of the finest politicians money can buy.

- Her job is a political plum. And we all know that it takes careful grafting to create a political plum.

- He's the perfect politician, with a dramatically straightforward way of dodging issues.

- I have only one piece of advice for her—in the words of Adlai Stevenson, "He who slings mud usually loses ground."

- He's a radical. As Franklin D. Roosevelt said, "A radical is a man with both feet planted firmly in the air."

- She'd better watch out for Marty Feldman who said, "I won't eat anything that has intelligent life, but I would gladly eat a network executive or a politician."

- The President has made a cabinet post for him: Secretary of the Inferior.

# PROCRASTINATORS

- She's not the greatest at paying her bills. We weren't surprised when the baby was overdue.

- We call her the great trombonist: She's always letting things slide.

(Authors' note: We meant to put more roasts in this category, but we didn't get around to it.)

# PROFESSIONS

## Accountants/Bookkeepers

- We asked her for proof that she was a bookkeeper and she brought in five books that were two years overdue at the library.

- He's one of the most creative people I know—when it comes to accounting.

- In her case, CPA stands for Constant Pain in the Ass.

- Everybody thinks he's a bit weird because he goes around with his fly open, but there's a legitimate reason—it's in case he has to count to eleven.

## Actors

- Marlon Brando, who ought to know, said it best, "An actor's a guy who if you ain't talking about him, he ain't listening."

- He wants to be a celebrity. I can't wait to see how he handles stardom. In fact, I think he'd probably be the perfect model for Fred Allen's description of a celebrity. He said, "A celebrity is a person who works hard all his life to become known, then wears dark glasses to avoid being recognized."

- She's always talking about her latest movie or her latest husband.

- Such a great actor. Who else could play Frankenstein without makeup.

- Earlier in her career, she was such a bad actor that when she played Lady Godiva, the horse got better reviews.

- He used to be such a bad actor that once, when his act followed Bongo the famous ape, the audience thought it was an encore.

- Some really good actors can stop a show. He's good at slowing it down.

- The only reason he wasn't hissed off the stage is that the audience couldn't yawn and hiss at the same time.

- Let's face it, the only reason she chose the field of acting is so she can sleep late.

- He's not just an actor—he's also a lover. And, as Wilson Mizner said, "Some of the greatest love affairs I've known involved one actor, unassisted."

- She needs to perform. She's even volunteered for police lineups.

- She's the only actress I know who went to Hollywood and slept with the writers.

## Advertising Executives

- Sometimes I wondered if the guy had the makings of an entrepreneur. Once he was really gung ho on a project he described as a funeral parlor for the twenty-first century. Unfortunately, he scared his investors away when he insisted on calling it Death 'N Things.

- She's just like the commercials she makes—loud and repetitive.

- He's an advertiser—or, as they used to say in the old days, a liar.

# Anesthesiologists

- He's so boring that when he took a career aptitude test, they said he should be an anesthesiologist.
- Anesthesiology. What a great career. They pay you to pass gas.

# Astronomers

- Clearly a natural astronomer—so spaced.
- She's meant for astronomy—what a heavenly body.
- He told his children they could watch the solar eclipse, but not to get too close.

# Bankers

- He's as generous as the banker about whom Robert Frost once said, "He'll lend you an umbrella in fair weather and ask for it back when it begins to rain."
- It's hard for me to trust bankers to count properly. If they could count, banks wouldn't always have eleven windows and three tellers.
- She thinks withdrawal pains are what happens to a bank when people take their money out.
- With him it's always a matter of principal—and interest.
- I know the two words she hates most: *free checking*.

# Carpenters

- He's a dedicated carpenter—always getting hammered.
- She's a natural carpenter—always chiseling.
- No wonder he's such a poor carpenter—he can't measure. He told me this [note: hold fingers two inches apart] was ten inches.
- Carpentry. What a job. He gets paid for screwing and sawing wood.

# Chiropractors

- She always complains that her work is backbreaking.
- He gets a lot more back pay—in fact, all his income is back pay.

# Clergy

- Father, your sermons are like water to a drowning man.
- Father, each of your sermons is better than the next.

# Coaches

- He treats all players the same—like dogs.
- We tried to get the coach gardening, but he couldn't stand the idea of the flowers being in their beds all of the time.

# Comedians

- She's always been funny. At least as far as looks go.
- He's not losing his touch. As Chevy Chase once said, "Bob Hope is as funny as he ever was. I just never thought Bob Hope was that funny in the first place."
- The only funny lines he has are on his face.

# Computer Experts

- He uses his technical knowledge to vastly increase his impact. As Paul Erlich said, "To err is human, but to really foul things up requires a computer."

- She started her career as a computer expert by adding extra holes to punch cards.

- I once called him with a computer question, and he started talking about IBM, CPUs, and a bunch of other TLAs (three-letter acronyms). So I replied, "Look you SOB, my system needs TLC, PDQ. So get your butt over here, ASAP!"

## Construction Workers

- He comes home every day and says his work was riveting.

- We knew she was a welder—she was always carrying a torch.

## Consultants

- She's a consultant, an expert. And Nicholas Murray Butler defined an expert as, "One who knows more and more about less and less."

- He's an expert—and we know how he got to be one. As Niels Bohr said, "An expert is a man who has made all the mistakes which can be made, in a narrow field."

## Dentists

- He's the guy that tells his patients to put their money where their mouth is.

- She specializes in removing wisdom teeth—jealousy, I guess.

# Dermatologists

- A woman's face is his fortune.

- He's always interested in the latest wrinkle.


# Diplomats

- Her definition of diplomacy is skating on thin ice without getting into deep water.

- A diplomat is an honest man sent abroad to lie for his country.

- She is the perfect diplomat, because she knows how to take something and act as though she were giving it away.

- He's got the selective memory needed to be a diplomat. As Robert Frost said, "A diplomat is a man who always remembers a woman's birthday but never remembers her age."

- As the ideal diplomat, she thinks twice before saying nothing.


# Directors

- He's the kind of director who likes to use real bullets in his movies.

- She once told an actor he had the right body for the part—and he was auditioning for voice-over talent.


# Disc Jockies

- She was made for radio—she's much too ugly to be seen.

- He's not much of an announcer—he learned his technique from Marcel Marceau.

# Doctors

- When they say she practices medicine, they're trying to warn you. She doesn't have it down yet—she's still practicing.

- He believes in homeopathetic medicine.

- I'm not impressed that she's a doctor. As Benjamin Franklin said, "God heals and the doctor takes the fee."

- He felt it was easier to become a doctor than a pharmacist, because he couldn't, for the life of him, figure out how they fit those little bottles in the typewriter.

- All doctors are really acupuncturists: They're always trying to stick it to their patients.

- I had hurt my leg, but she promised to get me walking quickly and she did; she took my car.

- Actually, obstetricians and storks have something in common: enormous bills.

- None of her patients live to regret choosing her.

- He became a bone specialist because his professors told him he had a head for it.


# Editors

- I share Adlai Stevenson's opinion of editors. He said, "An editor is a man who separates the wheat from the chaff and prints the chaff."

- She works in publishing, where the only remaining side benefit is the ability to sell books secondhand.

- He's a compulsive proofreader . . . and if it's not at least eighty proof, he's not interested in it.

# Engineers

- Engineers are smart in some things—and dumb in others. During the French Revolution, an engineer was due to be executed after a priest. The guillotine blade stopped halfway down, so they took it as a miracle and let the priest go. Then it was the engineer's turn. But before they could start he said, "Wait a minute, I see the problem."

- He has a two hundred dollar electrical bill—just for recharging his calculator.

# Entrepreneurs

- Why did she cross the road? To franchise the other side.

- Sometimes I wondered if the guy had the makings of an entrepreneur. Once he was really gung ho on a project he described as a funeral parlor for the twenty-first century. Unfortunately, he scared his investors away when he insisted on calling it Death 'N Things.

- His father, who ran a store, taught him everything about business. And he hasn't forgotten a word his father said: He still never gives anyone credit.

- She's quite the entrepreneur. She heard that the dollar's value was decreasing and the price of bread was going up, so she saved bread.

- His business is looking up—it's flat on its back.

- Her operations are basically sound—sound asleep.

- Her first word was *buy*.

- He's a self-made man who looks more like a warning than an example.

- She's a self-made woman who makes you wonder whether she's boasting or apologizing.

- Her motto is: If at first you don't succeed, buy, buy again.

# Fire Fighters

- The guy is such a committed firefighter that if he had twins he'd probably name them Jose [note: pronounced Hose A] [pause] and Hose B.

- It figures that he'd find a job that involved pulling long hoses.

- We call him the fireman—he's always chasing old flames.

- He decided to become a fireman when the local priest told him to go to blazes.

# Gamblers

- He was setting up a race for three year olds. Some parents will do anything.

- She thinks that 9 to 5 is a reasonable set of odds.

- He'll bet anyone 5 to 1 that he can quit gambling.

# Geologists

- His problem was that he took everything for granite.

- We call her the earthquake geologist: She's always finding faults.

# Insurance Salespeople

- He keeps trying to sell me a two hundred dollar debatable policy.

- She helps keep you poor so that you can die rich.

- The only advantage to getting old is that creeps like him will stop trying to sell me life insurance.

- Talk about a hard sell, this woman is the toughest. Why, just the other day, I heard her talking on the phone to a potential client. Her conversation went like this: "Hey, don't let me pressure you, Mrs. Schmidt. Take all the time in the world. In fact, why don't you sleep on my offer and call me in the morning. If you wake up."

• The policies he sells are so old they cover fire, theft, and Indian raids.

## Lawyers

• I don't know how this woman passed her bar exam. For the longest time, she thought an antitrust suit was a chastity belt.

• She's the quintessential divorce lawyer. To drum up business, she sent out fifteen hundred perfumed valentines signed, "Guess who?"

• He's the only person I know who hates bachelors. Why? He feels they're good-for-nothing assholes who cheat deserving women out of their divorce settlements.

• He's a typical lawyer, as defined by Lord Brougham who said, "A lawyer is a learned gentleman who rescues your estate from your enemies and keeps it himself."

• She may not know the law—but she generally knows the judge.

• As a lawyer, he can swim safely through shark-infested waters. Why? Professional courtesy.

• You can tell when she's lying: Her lips are moving.

• He may be a lawyer—but watch out if he offers to help you with your briefs.

• It took her a while to get used to being a lawyer. When she first started, she walked up to a prosecutor and said, "Do you have to make a federal case out of everything?"

## Massage Therapists

• She failed as a masseuse—she was always rubbing people the wrong way.

• He's not the best. No one told him he needed hands-on training.

# Meteorologists

- The only reason he became a meteorologist is because he thought he'd have a better chance of getting a hurricane named after him.

- Even when she was in high school, the boys could always look in her eyes and tell whether.

- He's got the only job on earth where you get paid for being right 50 percent of the time.

# Nurses

- It's easy to tell she's the head nurse. She's the only one with dirt on her knees.

- Her idea of being a practical nurse is marrying a rich patient.

- He's becoming an emergency-room nurse because he's better off wearing a mask.

# Pilots

- He's a great pilot, but he'll never get a chance to test-fly something like the Stealth bomber. Why? Because he'd be too busy honking the horn, squealing the tires, and playing the radio.

- She's a born pilot: flighty and always up in the air.

# Professors

- He's a professor—and you know what W. H. Auden said, "A professor is one who talks in someone else's sleep."

- She's a typical professor. She never had the guts to leave school and get a real job.

# Psychiatrists/Psychologists

- Here's to the psychiatrist: She finds you cracked and leaves you broke.

- He loves to work with nymphomaniacs, because a couch is a large part of their troubles.

- She thinks any woman who goes to a male psychologist should have her head examined. Why should she lie down on a man's couch, and then pay him?

- He's so indecisive, when a patient asked him if he had trouble making up his mind, he answered, "Yes and no."

- Talk about bad bedside manner, she's famous for telling her patients, "You haven't got an inferiority complex—you're inferior."

- He has such a split personality, his shrink had to get a sectional couch for him.

- She's so expensive, for seventy-five dollars all a patient gets is a get-well card.

- He practices a new kind of shock treatment—he sends his bill in advance.

- The poor woman is really married to her profession. Why just the other day she was walking down the street and met a fellow psychiatrist, and you know what she said? "You're fine—how am I?"

- It's like what Mervyn Stockwood said, "A psychiatrist is a man who goes to the Follies Bergere and looks at the audience." [or, for you plebeians]: You can always tell the shrinks—when a woman with big boobs walks into the room, they watch everyone else.

# Public Relations Consultants

- She's a public relations girl. Her biggest job is keeping her relations from becoming public.

- Every week he calls me with a new once-in-a-lifetime story.

- She's a genius: She can give anything a good image—except herself.

# Real Estate Brokers

- The man is obsessed. I asked him why he was so quiet once, and he said he had a *lot* on his mind.
- She's gotten quite fancy for a broker, she no longer makes house calls.

# Restaurateurs

- At his place, the tables are reserved, but the customers aren't.
- If you eat at her restaurant, don't ask for the specialty of the house: She's it.

# Salespeople

- Every week he calls me with a new once-in-a-lifetime opportunity.
- She's not guilty of sins of omissions—but the sins of commission will get her.
- Talk about a hard sell, this guy is the toughest. Why just the other day I heard him talking on the phone to a potential client. His conversation went something like this: "Hey, don't let me pressure you, Mrs. Schmidt. Take all the time in the world. In fact, why don't you sleep on my offer and call me in the morning. If you wake up."
- He's the kind of guy who wants to sell penicillin as "the perfect gift for someone who has everything."
- If she could sell cancer—she would.

# Scientists

- He's the only guy I know who uses a beaker, a flask, a retort, and a pipette to make a martini.
- He loves working with mice and rats—he says they all look up to him.

## Stockbrokers

- Her motto is: If at first you don't succeed, buy, buy again.
- He's always in the market for something . . . sometimes for investments.
- She doesn't get upset when she loses money—as long as it isn't her money.
- He normally plays below par—in his investments.
- After working with her, it's easy to see why they call the position "broker."
- It's easy to make a small fortune with him; all you need to start with is a large fortune.
- She's the only stockbroker I know who has a phobia about riding in elevators. She can't stand it when the operator says, "Going down."
- He made a friend of mine a millionaire—of course, my friend used to be a multimillionaire.

## Teachers

- He's a perfect example of George Bernard Shaw's quote, "He who can, does. He who cannot, teaches."
- What a hypocrite. She goes around saying that education pays, when one look at her salary tells you it doesn't.

## Veterinarians

- We've always known he would become a vet. When he was a teenager, he used to go out with some real dogs.
- She would have become a doctor, but she needed to work with patients who couldn't tell on her.

# Writers

- As Groucho Marx once told an author, "From the moment I picked up your book up until I laid it down, I was convulsed with laughter. Someday I intend to read it."

- He gets more rejections from publishers than anyone I know. I think Dr. Samuel Johnson summed up our guest of honor's problem best when he once told an author, "Your manuscript is both good and original; but the part that is good is not original and the part that is original is not good."

- She's not so hard to take. You just need the right attitude. As Michael Joseph said, "Authors are easy enough to get on with—if you are fond of children."

- He comes from a family of creative writers. His sister writes poetry, his mother writes short stories, and his father writes books. What does he write? Bad checks.

# PROMOTIONS & AWARDS

- I'm sure she'll have a few choice words to say when she accepts the award. She's like the great impromptu speaker Winston Churchill. F. E. Smith once said that "Winston devoted the best years of his life to preparing his impromptu speeches."

- His promotion hasn't changed him. He's still the same conniving SOB he's always been.

- As you rise in the world, it will do you good to remember the advice of Quentin Crisp who said, "Never keep up with the Joneses. Drag them down to your level. It's cheaper."

- As Dorothy Parker once said to a friend who had just given birth, "Congratulations: We all knew you had it in you."

111

# PUBLIC SPEAKING

- As a speaker, he gives you in length what he lacks in depth.
- Her speeches are like the horns of a steer—a point here, a point there, and a lot of bull in between.
- I'm sure he'll have a few choice words to say when he accepts the award. He's like the great impromptu speaker Winston Churchill. F. E. Smith once said that "Winston devoted the best years of his life to preparing his impromptu speeches."
- When she finally finishes her speech, there's a great awakening.
- He's the only person I know who gets a second wind as soon as he says, "In closing. . . ."
- She needs no introduction—what she needs is a conclusion.
- His audiences not only keep looking at their watches, they shake them.
- Her speeches are so long winded, she doesn't need a watch, she needs a calendar.
- He's the only speaker who always gets a silent ovation.
- I won't say what her speeches do to audiences, but Brahms's Lullabye is getting jealous.
- He's such an optimist, he puts his shoes on when a speaker says, "Now, in conclusion . . ."
- He took a public speaking class taught by Marcel Marceau.

# PUSSYWHIPPED

- He was quite a dude before he got married. Now he's subdued.
- He's not on good speaking terms with his girlfriend—but he's on great listening terms.

- When she wants his opinion, she gives it to him.

- He comes right out and says what she tells him to think.

- They are two minds with but a single thought—hers.

- He has the courage of her convictions.

- The last big decision she let him make was whether to wash or dry.

- He went home last night and gave his wife a good listening to.

- He and his wife have a way of coming to a compromise. He admits that he's wrong, and she forgives him.

- He put a ring on her finger, and she put a ring through his nose.

- He once found his best friend in bed with his wife and said, "Look, buddy, I have to, but you?"

- After an argument, they always patch things up—his jaw, his nose, his head . . .

- A friend once asked him what he did before he was married. And he answered with a sigh and a far-away look in his eyes: "Anything I wanted."

- You can tell who wears the pants in the family. Hell, the poor guy can't even commit suicide without asking his wife's permission.

- The good news is he's been given two weeks to live, the bad news is that's how long his wife is going to be away on vacation.

- He's a man of strong opinions—after he knows what his wife thinks.

- He never argues with her. He might win and then he's really in trouble.

- On the job application where it said marital status, he wrote, "Below wife."

- He really knows his place. When he disagrees with his wife, he puts his foot down and says, "No—and that's semifinal!"

# RELIGION

- He's religious, but in his own way. As John Bright said about Benjamin Disraeli, "He is a self-made man and worships his creator."

- She takes God for granted. She's like Heinrich Heine whose last words were "God will forgive me: That's his trade."

- He's made me a believer in reincarnation. Nobody could get as stupid as he is in just one lifetime.

- Don't give her credit for being too religious. As Joey Adams said of Robert Kennedy, "Robert Kennedy has a vigorous image—he has ten children. Everybody thinks that's because he's a devout Catholic. Not so—he's a sex maniac."

- Given his age, when he makes a donation to the church it's not a donation, it's an investment.

- She's deeply religious—she worships money.

# RESPONSIBILITY, LACK OF

- He's very responsible . . . whenever something goes wrong, he's responsible.

- She plays an essential role here—like a lifeguard at a carwash.

- His health is endangered when you lend him money—it damages his memory.

- She has a sure-fire way of handling temptation—she yields to it.

- He's not such a bad guy, or as Simone Signoret said of Jack Warner, "He bore no grudge against those he had wronged."

# RETIREMENT

- Watching you leave us behind with all of the work, I can only think of the heroic last words that the great explorer Richard Halliburton signaled from his sinking ship: "Southerly gales, squalls, lee rail under water, wet bunks, hard tack, bully beef, wish you were here—instead of me."

- Her retirement is typical of all her deals: She gets a pension, and the rest of us still get to work.

- She's been with our firm for over thirty years. No other firm wanted her.

- We're not sure what we'll do without him, but we've been dreaming about it for years.

- We won't forget him when he's long gone from the company . . . we'll forget him before he's out the door.

- His retirement will cause chaos. He kept his job all these years by keeping things so mixed up they couldn't fire him.

# REVENGE

- His philosophy of forgiveness comes from the great German poet and genius Heinrich Heine who wrote, "One should forgive one's enemies, but not before they are hanged."

- She's given us all something to live for: revenge.

- If you think women aren't explosive, try dropping one.

# RICH

- He's so rich, he has an unlisted wife.

- She doesn't count her money: She measures it.

- His wallet has bills in it with pictures of Presidents that I've never even heard of.

- She cashed a check and the bank bounced.

- There are dangers of being as rich as our guest. As Vic Braden once said of Bjorn Borg, "The only way he is going to hurt his arm is carrying his wallet."

# SCHOOL DAZE

- He went to an Ivy League school—so he can write on bathroom walls in Latin.

- She's so dumb that during her drug-experimenting days in college, she snorted NurtaSweet thinking it was Diet Coke.

- In college, he studied glass blowing—and he still blows every job he gets.

- She was pretty popular at college. Heck, she was voted The Girl with Whom You Are Most Likely to Succeed.

- Most of us had to decide what we were going to do once we got out of college and entered the real world. Not him. He's going to work for the government.

- In college, no one could understand why she didn't like sex until one day she confided in me. Turned out she just hated writing all those pesky thank-you notes.

- His dad backed his college education with thousands of dollars, and all he got was a quarterback.

- When she was in college, she was such a prude her roommates gave her a year's supply of cross-your-heart bras and no-nonsense stockings.

- One reason he went to [insert college/university] is so he could put his diploma on the car's dashboard and park in handicapped parking spots without getting a ticket.

- She comes from ——— where the old values are still important. At her grade school, for example, you had to raise your hand before you hit the teacher.

- Don't make too much out of the fact that he finally finished college. As Jack E. Leonard said of Joe Namath, he "spent four years in high school at the University of Alabama."

# SELF-DEPRECATION

- I tried to get her to make her morning tea in the microwave, but she still uses a kettle. She says that way at least something whistles at her.

- You got to admit, he knows his limitations. Once, while we were watching this guy step into his white, chauffeur-driven, stretch-Mercedes limousine, he said, "There but for me go I."

- He likes to steer clear of any talk about his family history. In fact, he'd be the first to agree with Fred Allen who once said, "I don't want to look up my family tree because I know I'm the sap."

- She's aged, and I'd bet she'd be the first to admit it. She'd also probably agree with Lucille Ball who once said, "I have everything I had twenty years ago—only it's all a little bit lower."

# SELF-IMPROVEMENT

- She's been in so many self-help programs, she thinks LA stands for Losers Anonymous.

- Even Robert Bly rejected him.

- She's going to quit drinking. It hasn't affected her health yet, but she can see the writing on the floor.

- We've all watched as he sought to find himself—and all wondered how he would deal with the inevitable disappointment.

- She's a compulsive self-improver. She's started to take ballet so she can stay on her toes.

- I don't really like telling stories out of school, but I heard his penis transplant didn't take. Turned out his hand rejected it.

- She's always out to improve herself. Every day she reads until her lips get tired.

# SEX

- He practiced the rhythm method—until his wife got tired of having a drummer in the bedroom.

- The poor guy's getting old, all right. How do I know? Well, just the other day he told me that his wife had given up sex for Lent and he didn't find out till Easter.

- He was going to get a vasectomy, but the doctor said to let sleeping dogs lie.

- In college, no one could understand why she didn't like sex until one day she confided in me. Turned out she just hated writing all those pesky thank-you notes.

- Don't be fooled. If she closes her eyes during sex, she's probably pretending she's shopping.

- She's not the sexiest woman I know. From what I understand, her version of foreplay is an hour of begging.

- He's so dumb that at the height of passion, if the woman was to whisper lustily that she wants to feel his throbbing muscle, he'd stop everything and roll up his sleeve.

- This woman gives a whole new definition to *sex kitten*. You know what I've heard she likes to say just before she climaxes? "Sorry Mom, I've got to hang up now. . . ."

- He and Rodney Dangerfield have something in common. And Rodney described it best when he said, "My wife wants her sex in the back seat of a car—but she wants me to drive."

- They bought a waterbed, but her side kept freezing.

- She enjoys movies so much, you'd think the previews were foreplay.

- He holds several speed records—unfortunately they are for sexual events.

- If only his zipper could talk.

- He's a practical romantic. Although he hasn't gotten married yet, he's found solace in Woody Allen's observation that "Love is the answer, but while you are waiting for the answer, sex raises some pretty good questions."

- She has a good grasp of her own sexuality; and that's the only sex she gets.

- His wife put a mirror over the bed—she likes to watch herself laugh.

- Here's to ———,
  for whom life held no terrors.
  Born a virgin, died a virgin;
  no hits, no runs, no errors.

- Every year he plays Santa Claus. It makes the kids feel so happy—and he gets to feel normal—because Santa is only expected to come once a year.

- We're talking an avid reader here. She keeps three books by the bed. One for when she's trying to get to sleep, one for when she wakes up and can't sleep, and one for spare moments during sex.

# SEXISTS

- When I'm asked about her performance at work, I always respond with Dr. Johnson's comment on a woman preaching. He said it is "like a dog walking on his hind legs. It is not well done; but you are surprised to find it done at all."

- He's the kind of guy that inspired Madame de Staël to say, "The more I see of men, the more I like dogs."

- He's all for electing a woman for vice president. And why shouldn't he be, because the way he sees it, they wouldn't have to pay her as much.

- He's quite the understanding male. Once, while making love, his girlfriend screamed, "Stop! It hurts!" and Mr. Sensitive replied, "Yo, you're crazy. It feels great."

- The guy is so macho, I'll bet he was circumcised with pinking shears.

- Just looking at him, I can tell that sex with this man would probably be akin to poetry in motion. Something along the lines of: Slam, bam, thank you ma'am.

- Macho? Hell, he's so macho he'd probably jog home from his own vasectomy.

- She's a liberated woman, and I like that. In fact, I'm all for women's liberation. I think it's about time you girls had something to do in your spare time.

- He's such a romantic, his idea of foreplay is to look adoringly into his partner's eyes and whisper, "Don't scream or I'll kill you."

- Why did God create this wonderful bride for this lucky groom? Easy. Sheep can't cook.

# SLOBS

- She's never made it into *Who's Who*; but she's in *What's That*.

- He's a slob all right, but I wouldn't go as far as to say he's an ape. It's not really fair to the apes, because an ape at least peels a banana before he eats it.

- She's a slob. In fact, I've heard that the only time she ever washes her ears is when she's eating from the middle of a large slice of watermelon.

- He's mean, selfish, loudmouthed, and uncouth, but in spite of all that, there's something about him that repels you.

- I don't think cleaning is one of her priorities. I once asked her if she was going to straighten up her house, and she said, "Why? Is it tilted?"

- She doesn't mind if her hair looks like a mop, especially since she has no idea what a mop looks like.

- His closet would be a pig's sty even if he lived in a nudist colony.

- The only time she looks just right is on Halloween.

- She's got the only car I've ever seen that has roaches.

# SMOKING

- The good news is he's finally quit smoking. The bad news is he's getting slapped by his dates more often, because he needs something to do with his hands.

- She read so much about the evils of smoking that she decided to give up reading.

- He's a big cigar smoker. And you know what cigars are—breath fresheners for people who eat shit.

- Her family and friends don't mind if she smokes. In fact, they don't mind if she burns.

- I wouldn't say he's addicted to smoking, but he once traded his mother for a pack of Virginia Slims.

# SNOBS

- She's a snob. Just like Nancy Reagan, about whom Joey Adams said, "Nancy has this recurring nightmare—she's kidnapped, taken to A&S, and forced to buy dresses right off the rack."

- He loves the working man; he loves to see them work.

- She would avoid her inferiors, if she could find any.

- His nose is so high in the air, every time he sneezes, he sprays the ceiling.

- She's a snob all right. You know how she was weaned? Her mother fired the maid.

- He's open minded, all right. You know what his idea of mass transit is? The ferry to Martha's Vineyard.
- Her idea of open-mindedness is dating a Canadian.
- You know what he said to me after I accused him of being affected? "Who? *Moi?*"

# SPENDERS, BIG

- He really brightens up the office—he never turns off the lights.
- She had her purse stolen, but her husband hasn't reported the lost credit cards—the thief is spending less than she did.
- Her husband is real generous. When she asks him for clothes money, he tells her to go to the best shops and pick something nice—just don't get caught.
- She went window shopping and bought a dozen windows.
- You know what her favorite sexual position is? Facing Bloomingdale's.
- Don't be fooled. If she closes her eyes during sex, she's probably pretending she's shopping.
- She has two big complaints: She has nothing to wear and she needs more closet space.
- They have a joint checking account. She puts in the money, and he takes it out.
- He's four years ahead of his time. In 1992, he'd already spent his salary for 1996.
- She made a friend of mine a millionaire—of course, my friend used to be a multimillionaire.

# SPORTS

## Baseball/Softball

- He's already in training for next year's baseball season—he's got the spitting and scratching part down.

- She would rather steal hubcaps than second base.

- He's so sneaky, he could steal third base with his foot on second.

## Basketball

- He needs to remember what his mother used to say when she put him to bed: "No palming."

- She eats the way she plays basketball: always dribbling.

- He plays basketball so much that he takes it as a compliment when he's told to stuff it.

## Bowling

- He has unique technique. He's one of the few adults I've ever seen who uses two arms.

- She's a dedicated bowler—a real pin head.

- He's a dedicated bowler—his mind is always in the gutter.

## Boxing

- If you're standing next to him, don't order punch.

- We call him Picasso, because he's always working on canvas.

- Talk about tough, he was in a fight recently and scared the hell out of his opponent. The poor guy thought he had killed him.

- He's very superstitious. Before he goes into a fight, he puts a horseshoe in his boxing glove.

- He was knocked out so often he sold advertising space on the soles of his shoes.

- He's so old he can remember a pro boxing match between two white guys.

## Exercise

- He definitely takes a short cut when it comes to exercising. Every morning, instead of bending over and touching his toes with his fingers, he touches them with his stomach.

- Look at her. She's in such terrible shape, if she ran a bath, she'd come in second.

- He's in such awful shape, when he sits down he looks like batter spreading.

- She's amazing. She's the only one I know who tries to contract athlete's foot—she thinks if she gets it people will treat her like a jock.

- The only exercise he gets is running people down, sidestepping responsibilities, and putting his foot in his mouth.

- The only regular exercise she gets is pushing her luck.

- He holds several speed records—unfortunately they are for sexual events.

- Her idea of stretching exercises is stretching the truth.

- Her idea of exercise is jumping to conclusions.

- His main problem with aerobics is that he can't count high enough to check his training rate.

# Fishing

- He's not much at fly fishing, but he's a Master Baiter.

- She feels challenged by fish—she thinks of fishing as a battle of wits.

- We were going fishing and we told her to bring a pole—she brought some guy named Stanislav.

- It's not that he lies about the size of his fish on purpose—his wife says he's never known the difference between six inches and a foot.


# Football

- His dad supported his college education with thousands of dollars, and all he got was a quarterback.

- I think Lyndon Baines Johnson said it best about our football hero over here when he described Gerry Ford as "a nice guy, but he played too much football with his helmet off."

- Our football star finally finished college, but I use that term loosely. As Jack E. Leonard said of Joe Namath, he "spent four years in high school at the University of Alabama."

- He comes from ——— where they had to put Astroturf into the stadium to keep the cheerleaders from grazing at halftime.


# Golf

- She missed a hole in one by only three strokes.

- He can play a much better round of golf now. He can go around in a little less than a quart.

- He's a two-handicap golfer—he has a boss who won't let him off early, and a wife who won't let him out.

- I don't know if any of you are aware of it, but [name] once broke his leg playing golf. He fell off the ball wash.
- She's the only golfer who falls asleep during her own backswing.
- God invented golf so guys like [name] could dress like like pimps.
- He normally plays below par—in his investments.
- He's too fat to play golf. If he puts the ball where he can hit it, he can't see it, and if he puts it where he can see it, he can't hit it.

## Gymnastics

- She's so limber she could literally bend over backwards for you.
- Don't tell him to kiss his ass—he can probably can do it.

## Horseback Riding

- She likes the feel of something big, strong, warm, and hairy between her legs. She also likes to go riding.
- He's so dumb, he thinks the Kentucky Derby is a hat.

## Hunting

- Talk about your great white hunter, this guy was driving along and came to a sign that said BEAR LEFT. So what did he do? He went home.
- You'd think this guy was really politically correct because he won't go elephant hunting. I know differently. The only reason he quit hunting elephants is because he had a difficult time carrying the decoys.

## Jogging/Running

- He's always running. Unfortunately, he keeps coming back.
- Look at her. She's in such terrible shape, if she ran a bath, she'd come in second.

- The only thing fast about him is his watch.

- She's so lazy, when she gets a cold even her nose won't run.

- Him a runner? Huh! The only thing that runs around his house is the fence.

## Martial Arts

- He has learned the ancient Oriental defense method of screaming and begging.

- She thinks judo is what you use to make bagels.

## Motorcycling

- Let's face it, he'd go for any sport that lets him wear full leathers.

- He sits on his bike, and you hear all sorts of powerful bubbling noises. Then he turns the engine on.

## Ping-Pong

- He could have been a serious Ping-Pong player if he'd just stop jumping over the net every time he won.

- She's so out of it, she thinks Ping-Pong is a city in China.

## Pool

- She's not sure why she likes the game so much. Something about long hard sticks and big round balls.

- He and a cue ball have a lot in common—both can be found stuck behind the eight ball.

## Pro Athletes

- He's an athlete, but not a gentleman. As Gordie Howe said, "All pro athletes are bilingual. They speak English and profanity."

- The man's rolling in dough. As Vic Braden said about tennis great, Bjorn Borg, "The only way he is going to hurt his arm is carrying his wallet."

## Racquetball

- He spends more time in court than most lawyers.

- She's comfortable on a racquetball court—she should be, it's bigger than her apartment.

## Sailing

- He's really into sailing. And you know what a sailboat is: A floating box you throw money into.

- Sailing's the sport for her. She really likes seamen.

- When I think of his sailing exploits, I can only think of the heroic last words that the great explorer Richard Halliburton signaled from his sinking ship: "Southerly gales, squalls, lee rail under water, wet bunks, hard tack, bully beef, wish you were here—instead of me."

## Scuba Diving/Skin Diving/Snorkeling

- Leave it to her to find a sport where you have to get tanked.

- Of course, he would choose a hobby where you wear tight, black latex suits.

- Of course, she would choose a sport where you are always going down.

# Skiing

- Perfect sport for him: always going downhill.
- She has the latest quick-release bindings—on her bed.
- His staff is taking skiing lessons so they can go downhill with him.

# Surfing

- Her favorite trick is riding the board all the way to the beach. She calls it surf and turf.
- What an overachiever! He likes to hang eleven.

# Swimming

- She took swimming lessons from the guy who taught Natalie Wood.
- The only reason he manages to keep his head above water is that wood floats.
- She got started because she thought that the breast stroke and the butterfly were sexual techniques.
- He's spent years swimming. He should have used ear plugs, because you can hear water sloshing when he shakes his head.
- No wonder she swims so well. Shit floats.

# Tennis

- I thought I caught her talking business once. I heard the phrase *net results*—turned out that she was talking about tennis.
- He's perfect for a sport in which *love* means nothing.
- She likes tennis—it's the only time a girl like her gets to wear white.

## Track & Field

- His event is the pole vault, but he's more interested in broad jumping.
- She broke a sprint record—running away from the cops.

## Volleyball

- He needs to remember what his mother used to say when she put him to bed: "No palming."
- Even her drinks are spiked.
- It took him a while to get a grasp of the game of volleyball. He finally learned how the players rotate—and it only took four years.

## Waterskiing

- It was hard for her to learn to water ski. She's not used to keeping her legs together.
- Typical of him to get into a sport where someone else pulls you.

# STUBBORNNESS

- He never lets facts interfere with his opinion.
- Arguing with her is like trying to read a newspaper in a high wind.
- Arguing with him is like trying to blow out an electric light bulb.
- Her mind is usually made up, so don't confuse her with the facts.
- He's so opinionated, he won't even listen to both sides of a cassette.
- The narrower her mind, the broader her statements.

- You have as much chance of winning an argument with him as with an umpire.

- When she wants your opinion, she gives it to you.

- His mind is like concrete—all mixed up and permanently set.

- She knows her mind. When she reached forty, she definitely decided what she wanted to be—thirty-five.

# STUPID

- He should take up the study of space. He has the head for it.

- She was asked what she thought of Red China and she said, "It's all right as long as it doesn't clash with the tablecloth."

- His mind is as sharp as a marble.

- Anyone who would offer her a penny for her thoughts is definitely overpaying.

- He's made me a believer in reincarnation. Nobody could get as stupid as he is in just one lifetime.

- She's so stupid, she thought Johnny Cash was a pay toilet.

- He's so dumb that at the height of passion, if the woman was to whisper lustily that she wants to feel his throbbing muscle, he'd stop everything and roll up his sleeve.

- I love the guy, but he's so literal. Once, he took a leak right in the middle of a diner. When I asked him what the hell he was doing, he nonchalantly pointed at a sign that read, WET FLOOR.

- She's so dumb, she thinks Taco Bell is the Mexican phone company.

- He's the only person I know who thinks Moby Dick is a social disease, asphalt is a proctological condition, and that Ping-Pong balls are a Chinese venereal disease.

- One reason she went to [insert college/university] is so she could put her diploma on the car's dashboard and park in the handicapped parking spots without getting a ticket.

- Management doesn't give him more than an hour for lunch, because they don't want to have to retrain him.

- She's so dumb, if she were an elevator operator, she'd lose her job because she'd keep forgetting the route.

- I've always wondered how long one could live without a brain. Ahh, [name], how old are you again?

- I wouldn't say he was stupid or anything, but in order to keep him from hurting himself while working around the house, his wife had the word *STOP* stencilled on the top rung of his ladder.

- He's so dumb, he thinks the Kentucky Derby is a hat.

- She's so dumb, the reason she never bought a color TV is because she didn't know what color to get.

- He's so literal he thinks a briefcase is where you keep your underwear.

- She has to take her shoes off to count to twenty.

- If brains were gunpowder, she couldn't blow her nose.

- Compared to him, Dan Quayle is an intellectual.

- He has more intelligence in his little finger than he has in his big finger.

- She's so dumb, she studies for the pap test.

- He's a great soldier, but he's a bit dim. In his will, he's leaving all his money to the unknown soldier's widow.

- Blondes like her do have more fun—so little is expected of them.

- He's nice, but not of this world. He's kind of like Hugh Downs, about whom Joe Garagiola once said, "If Hugh woke up on Christmas day and found a pile of manure under the tree, he'd wonder where they were hiding the pony."

# STUPID, REALLY

- I've always wondered, when he changes his mind, what does he do with the diaper?

- I've worn dresses that have a higher IQ than she does.

- She dresses well, but as Harriet Fallon once said, "Her clothes are smarter than she is."

- He did one heck of a job training the new secretaries. In fact, you could tell which people he was directly responsible for. They were the ones with White-Out all over their computer screens.

- She was in the same grade so long, people were beginning to think she was the teacher.

- It was a great day when he graduated. The teachers cried for joy—they thought he'd never leave.

- He didn't stay for the second act of the play because it said on the program, "Act 2, a week later."

- She told her children they could watch the solar eclipse, but not to get too close.

- He's so stupid, the stork that brought him should have been arrested for smuggling dope.

- The poor guy was so frazzled after the doctor informed him that his wife had just given birth to twins, he got pissed off and went looking for the other fellow.

- Talk about your great white hunter, this guy was driving along and came to a sign that said BEAR LEFT. So what did he do? He went home.

- She's so boring, she can't even entertain a doubt.

- She's *Vogue* on the outside and vague on the inside.

- He should sue his brains for nonsupport.

- The poor woman is recovering from a bizarre accident. She was struck by a thought.

- I don't know about you people, but I feel sorry for that poor little mind all alone in that great big head.

- If he ever decided to expound on something he actually knew, the silence would be unbearable.

- She sings like a bird—and has a brain like one too.

- It would take a team of surgeons working many hours to get an idea into his head.

- The doctor once told her she had acute bronchitis, and she yelled back angrily, "Hey, buddy, I came here to be examined, not flattered."

- He once read a statistic that a man gets hit by a car every fifteen minutes. You know what his response was? "Boy, that guy must be a glutton for punishment."

- He stands in front of the mirror with his eyes closed to see what he looks like when he's asleep.

- The only thing that can stay in her head more than an hour is a cold.

- He lost his mind when a butterfly kicked him in the head.

- How would I describe our guest of honor? The expression that comes to mind is, the lights are on, but nobody's home.

- The only reason she manages to keep her head above water is that wood floats.

- It's not that he hasn't presence of mind; his trouble is absence of thought.

# STUPID, REALLY, REALLY

- He's so stupid, he thinks that *innuendo* is the Italian word for suppository.

- She's even stuck for an answer when someone says, "Hello."

- He has an open mind; a very open mind . . . O.K., his head is empty.

- She was so dumb, she thought dropsy was a problem that moving men had.

- It's not right to say that he's a perfect idiot. . . . No one's perfect.

- What she lacks in intelligence, she makes up for in stupidity.

- She doesn't know the meaning of the word *quit*. In fact, she doesn't know the meaning of most words.

- He breaks all the rules . . . like the one that says wisdom comes with age.

- She's brighter than she looks—she has to be.

- He's always out to improve himself. Every day he reads until his lips get tired.

- If she lived by her wits, she'd starve.

- He wanted to get into a duel of wits with me; but I refused to fight an unarmed opponent.

- She wanted to give me a piece of her mind, but I told her I didn't think she could spare it.

- He got drunk once and made a pass at me. He asked me to "screw his brains out." I told him it was too late for that.

- They don't serve ice at their house anymore—they lost the recipe.

- She went to a mind reader and was only charged half price.

- He broke his arm while raking leaves—he fell out of the tree.

- As Fred Allen said, "What's on your mind, if you will allow the over-statement?"

- What was it like to work with him? Well, as Heinrich Heine once said, "Ordinarily he was insane, but he had lucid moments when he was merely stupid."

- I found the perfect quote by Sigrid Undset that describes our guest of honor in a nut shell. Sigrid said, "He was not made for climbing the tree of knowledge."

- To use Francis Bradley's description, "His mind is open; yes, it is so open that nothing is retained; ideas simply pass through him."

- She'd better watch out for Marty Feldman who said, "I won't eat anything that has intelligent life, but I would gladly eat a network executive or a politician."

- How slow is he? As Edwin W. Edwards once said, "He's so slow that he takes an hour and a half to watch *60 Minutes*."

- If she said what she thought she'd be speechless.

- He has a soft heart—and a head to match.

- We knew she wasn't too bright when she won the toss at a track meet and elected to receive the javelin.

- What do Gerry Ford and our guest of honor have in common? Well, Lyndon Baines Johnson's quote about Gerry Ford summed it up nicely. He said, he's a "nice guy, but he played too much football with his helmet off."

- She has lots of fiber in her diet, and in her head.

- The only book he's ever finished is a book of matches.

- Don't make too much out of the fact that he finally finished college. As Jack E. Leonard said of Joe Namath, he "spent four years in high school at the University of Alabama."

- To call her stupid is an insult to stupid people.

- He's completely ignorant when it comes to baking. Once he attempted to make a pineapple upside-down cake and ended up getting a hernia. He tried to turn the oven over.

- She's a hard worker. She spent her whole lunch hour trying to alphabetize a bag of M&Ms. She did a great job. By the end of the hour, she had two groups—Ms and Ws.

- Those aren't acne scars on his face, he just had a hard time learning to eat with a fork.

- Everybody thinks he's a bit weird because he goes around with his fly open, but there's a legitimate reason—it's in case he has to count to eleven.

- She's the only actress I know who went to Hollywood and slept with the writers.

- His main problem with aerobics is that he can't count high enough to check his training rate.

- She brought her cosmetics to a make-up exam.

- He has something in common with his car—neither one fires on all cylinders.

- When she started, we told her Friday was filing day . . . she came in ready to do her nails.

- He's always ready to give an outsider's opinion of the human race.

- This woman is so smart, if you ask her to spell *Mississippi*, she'll snap right back with "the river or the state?"

- He's always out to improve himself. Every day he reads until his lips get tired.

- She was asked if she liked Kipling and she answered, "I don't know—I've never kippled."

- She's not what you'd call a born student: She flunked recess.

- The closest he's ever come to a brainstorm is a light drizzle.

- When he was in the fifth grade, he wasn't at all like any of the other kids—maybe that was because he was nineteen.

- When I think of our guest of honor, a John Dawkin quote comes immediately to mind. He said, "I heard his library burned down and that both books were destroyed—and one of them hadn't even been colored in yet."

# THIEVES

- She has a mind like a bolt of lightning: bright and fast, but very crooked.

- His shoes match his personality: sneakers and loafers.

- She knows a good joke when she steals one.

- He's worked in a lot of hotels—and he has the silverware and towels to prove it.

- She always has a lot of trouble with those fluffy, thick hotel towels—she can hardly close her suitcase.

- He gives publicly and steals privately.

- She likes to eat her cake and have yours too.

- He's so crooked, he has to screw his socks on.

- You're safe when he holds you tenderly with his hands—because at least you know where they are.

- She started out in life as an unwanted child—now she's wanted in ten states.

- He's so crooked, he can hide in the shadow of a corkscrew.

- She's so crooked, when she dies they'll have to screw her into the ground.

- He comes from a family of creative writers. His sister writes poetry, his mother writes short stories, and his father writes books. And he writes bad checks.

- She's done a good deal for lots of people. She's kept a flock of detectives, bill collectors, and Treasury men working regularly.

- As a young fellow, he once ran away with a circus, but the police caught him and made him bring it back.

- She got in trouble for something she didn't do—pay her taxes.

138

# UNCOUTH

- You know what's the difference between [name] and a bowl of yogurt? Yogurt has culture.

- She was asked what she thought of Red China and she said, "It's all right as long as it doesn't clash with the tablecloth."

- He thinks he's classy because he knows which fingers to put in his mouth when he whistles for the waiter.

- She doesn't just slurp her soup, she yodels it.

- One night, while dining out at a nightclub, he sipped his soup so loudly, ten couples got up to dance.

- She eats with her fingers and talks with her forks.

- He's a contact man—all con and no tact.

- He eats the way he plays basketball: always dribbling.

- She's like a school vacation: no class.

- You'd make a fortune if you could buy him for what you think of him, and sell him for what he thinks of himself.

- She was asked if she liked Kipling and she answered, "I don't know—I've never kippled."

- His idea of subtle was Liberace.

- Talk about tact. Her family has never told her why they really pray before each meal.

- He's a real class act. Last week he got into a cab and asked the driver if there was room in front for a pizza and a six-pack. Sure, said the driver obligingly. So what did he do? He opened the partition, leaned forward, and threw up.

- Watching the toe dancers at the ballet, she wanted to know why they didn't get taller girls.

- I love the guy, but he's so literal. Once he took a leak right in the middle of a diner. When I asked him what the hell he was doing, he nonchalantly pointed at a sign that read, WET FLOOR.

- Why does she have such a beautiful nose? Well, that's obvious. It's handpicked.

- He thinks you have to go to France to get plaster of paris.

# UNFITNESS

- His idea of exercise is jumping to conclusions.

- She's so out of shape, she gets winded when her stockings run.

- He's so out of shape, he gets winded playing checkers.

- She eats so much bran to stay healthy that she sways in the breeze.

- He's so far out of shape that chess is an aerobic sport.

- She's so out of shape the doctor makes her pay in advance.

- Looking at him, you can see that he lives by those immortal words of Robert Maynard Hutchins, who said, "Whenever I feel like exercise, I lie down until the feeling passes."

- There's not much you can say about his body. He's in as bad shape as Buddy Hackett, about whom Red Buttons said, he was "a man who willed his body to science, and science is contesting the will."

# UPTIGHT

- Her idea of a nymphomaniac is someone who has sex at least once a month.

- I wouldn't say he's inexperienced. It's just that when he lies on a waterbed, images of Lake Placid and the Dead Sea immediately come to mind.

- Her idea of perfect sex is simultaneous headaches.

- What's the difference between her and a volcano? Volcanoes don't fake eruptions.

- The only difference between her and a freezer is that you have to plug in a freezer.

- Come on, let's face it. The only difference between her and poverty is that poverty sucks.

- His idea of a dream house is eight rooms, no kitchen, no bedroom.

- When I heard that she did it doggie style, I was amazed. I hadn't realized she was so progressive. Then I found out what her definition of doggie style is; he gets on all fours and begs while she rolls over and plays dead.

- He's such a prude, he's embarrassed to admit he'd been born in bed—with a woman.

- I wouldn't say he's frigid. Let's just say he flunked puberty.

- His idea of open-mindedness is dating a Canadian.

- She's just a little too sweet for my taste. Just as Christopher Plummer said of Julie Andrews, "Working with her is like being hit over the head with a valentine's card."

- Don't get taken in by her act. I know better. I've known her longer than most. In the immortal words of Groucho Marx about Doris Day, "I've been around so long, I knew Doris Day before she was a virgin."

- He reminds me of William Faulkner's comment about Henry James, whom he called, "One of the nicest old ladies I ever met."

- He's such a prude. His idea of foreplay is drying the dishes.

- His definition of safe sex is foreplay.

- She's such a prude, she puts a condom on her vibrator.

- He's the only person I know who thinks Moby Dick is a social disease, asphalt is a proctological condition, and Ping-Pong balls are a Chinese venereal disease.

- When she was in college, she was such a prude her roommates gave

141

her a year's supply of cross-your-heart bras and no-nonsense stockings.

- She's so cold. She must be one of God's frozen people.

- The only thing fast about him is his watch.

- In college, no one could understand why she didn't like sex until one day she confided in me. Turned out she just hated writing all those pesky thank-you notes.

- His life is so slow, he actually looks forward to dental appointments.

- He wears a belt and suspenders—on his pajamas.

- Look at her sitting there all prim and proper. She reminds me of a quote by Lucille Ball about Jimmy Stewart. Lucy said, "Jimmy Stewart is sort of square. Even in the early days, he told me his idea of a romantic evening was soft lights, sweet music, champagne . . . no girl—just soft lights, sweet music, and champagne."

# WACKOS

- She says she has an inferiority complex, but most of us disagree—we feel that it's entirely justified.

- Come on, it's clear he doesn't have an inferiority complex. He's too simple to have anything complex.

- She goes into a public bathroom and changes the toilet paper roll so it rolls from the top, just the way she likes it. What's weird is that she changes the paper in all the stalls.

- He's so afraid of heights, he won't let the barber pump up the chair.

- She's not paranoid—the world really *is* out to get her.

- He's beside himself so much of the time, I think he's schizophrenic.

- She's so anal retentive she tries to alphabetize her soup.

- He's a manic depressive—easy glum, easy glow.

- When I look at her, I understand why Allen Ginsberg said, "I've seen the best minds of my generation destroyed by madness."

- No one in his family suffers from insanity—they all enjoy it.

- She has such a split personality, her shrink had to get a sectional couch for her.

- His psychiatrist is so expensive, all he gets for seventy-five dollars is a get-well card.

- Her shrink practices a new kind of shock treatment—he sends his bill in advance.

- He's so crazy that before his first session with the shrink was over, the psychiatrist had to get on the couch.

- Once it took three distinguished psychiatrists to discover what made her tick—and what made her chime on the hour and half hour.

- On his last day in therapy, the doctor congratulated him and told him his delusions were a thing of the past. "Great," answered the patient sadly, "yesterday I was Genghis Khan and today I'm a nobody."

- He's as nervous and jumpy as a long-tailed cat in a room full of rocking chairs.

- Her hair was straight before she started this job.

- He's so nervous, he keeps coffee awake.

- She'll never have a nervous breakdown, but she sure is a carrier.

# WIMPS

- He reminds me of William Faulkner's comment about Henry James, whom he called, "One of the nicest old ladies I ever met."

- He had to take steroids to be on the chess team.

- She's so pale, if she wanted to blush, she'd have to get a blood transfusion.

- He seems like the quiet type. Maybe he's what Winston Churchill described as "a sheep in sheep's clothing."
- Her idea of leadership is to find a parade and get in front of it.
- He's a regular rock of Jell-O.
- After they made her, they broke the Jell-O mold.
- He's so chicken, he needs an anesthetic just to sit in a dentist's waiting room.
- Her idea of roughing it is to turn her electric blanket down to low.
- Talk about tough, he was in a fight recently and scared the hell out of his opponent. The poor guy thought he had killed him.
- Once she makes up her mind, she's full of indecision.
- We call him Mr. Decisive: He's the guy you go to when you want a definite maybe.
- There are two sides to every question; and she always takes both.
- He's the perfect executive, with a dramatically straightforward way of dodging the issues.
- She never goes back on her word—without consulting her lawyer.
- He's so indecisive, when his psychiatrist asked him if he had trouble making up his mind, he answered, "Yes and no."
- She's so indecisive, she has a four-year-old son she hasn't named yet.
- He's a man of conviction—after he knows what his wife thinks.
- The only time she's sure where she's going is right after she gets an enema.
- As Mark Twain would say, "He would come in and say he changed his mind—which was a gilded figure of speech, because he didn't have any."
- And don't give him too much credit for being decent and having a clean mind. There's a reason for his pure thoughts. In the words of Oliver Herford, "His mind is cleaner than most—he changes it more often."

# WOMANIZERS

- He is improving his attitude towards women—just like Joe Namath. As Dean Martin once said of Broadway Joe, "He has great respect for girls. Only last week in New York, he saved a girl from being attacked. He controlled himself."

- If he was a girl, he'd be pregnant all the time.

- Some people tell business secrets to their wives. He's more dangerous; he tells business secrets to other men's wives.

- When this guy is horny, even the hair on the barbershop floor isn't safe.

- Errol Flynn had the same problem he has. Here's how Flynn described it: "My problem lies in reconciling my gross habits with my net income."

- If only his zipper could talk.

- He's a practical romantic. Although he hasn't gotten married yet, he's found solace in Woody Allen's observation that "Love is the answer, but while you are waiting for the answer, sex raises some pretty good questions."

- Hey, the guy's not that old. Give him a break. I know for a fact he still chases girls—unfortunately, it's only downhill.

- He tries to make every dollar—and every girl—go as far as possible.

- What do you give to a stud like this who has everything? Penicillin.

- If he could, he'd invent a morning-after pill for men. You know how it would work? It'd change your blood type.

- Thank God he's got a few more brains than a dog or he'd be arrested for humping women's legs at cocktail parties.

- He's quite the lady's man. In fact, women are amazed at how well he dresses and how quickly too.

- He may be a lawyer—but watch out if he offers to help you with your briefs.

- He's such a womanizer, he treats all women as sequels.

- He's real broad minded—in fact, he thinks of nothing else.

- He believes in nothing risqué, nothing gained.

- He's the friendly type—always inviting women up to his apartment for a Scotch and sofa.

- He goes around with more women than a revolving door.

- The way he dances, it looks like a vertical expression of a horizontal idea.

- He got beaten up fighting for a woman's honor. Seems she wanted to keep it.

- Last New Year's he made a solemn resolution to cut down on wine and women. It was the most miserable three hours of his life.

- Every time he goes out with a woman, he runs into the same old problem, either she's married or he is.

- He's still chasing women, but he can't remember why.

- He's going to have to keep an eye on his amorous activities. The way he chases a skirt, he's sure to wind up with a suit.

- He can't understand it when his friends ask him if he cheats on his wife. Who else is he going to cheat on?

- He's one of the few men who keeps his eyes open when he kisses a woman. Maybe that's because he's constantly on the lookout for his wife.

- Hey, nobody can accuse the guy of being thoughtless. Many times he's thought about taking a wife. His only problem is whose wife to take.

- He's frank and earnest with women. In Chicago he's Frank and in Denver he's Ernest.

# WORKERS, WORTHLESS

- He's like Jerome K. Jerome who once said, "I love work—I can watch it all day."

- Who says nothing is impossible. She's been doing nothing for years.

- He's not afraid of hard work—in fact, he can sleep right next to it.

- She thinks of her co-workers as family—she's always referring to them as mothers.

- My reaction to his memos is the same as King James I's reaction to John Donne's poetry. The king said, "Dr. Donne's verses are like the peace of God; they pass all understanding."

- Once she was sick in bed for a whole week, and her secretary sent a sympathy card to her husband.

- Believe it or not, he's known as a miracle worker—it's a miracle when he works.

- She's a real steady worker. If she gets any steadier, she'll be motionless.

- He's very consistent. Every day he works eight hours and sleeps eight hours—unfortunately, they're the same eight hours.

- She's a hard worker. She spent her whole lunch hour trying to alphabetize a bag of M&Ms. She did a great job. By the end of the hour, she had two groups—Ms and Ws.

- Her hair was straight before she started this job.

- Management doesn't give him more than an hour for lunch, because they don't want to have to retrain him.

- She did one heck of a job training the new secretaries. In fact, you could tell which people she was directly responsible for. They were the ones with Wite-Out all over their computer screens.

- He's a good worker, but he's easily confused. If you don't believe me, give him two shovels and tell him to take his pick.

- Her boss would love to pay her what she's worth, but there's a law against paying less than minimum wage.

- He was fired because he was lax about his appearance; he didn't show up most of the time.

- When she started, we told her Friday was filing day . . . she came in ready to do her nails.

- He can erase at eighty words a minute.

- She's learned many things while working with us: the alphabet, for one.

- She believed that it was part of her job as a maid to drink all the wine labelled *domestic*.

- He loves the working man; he loves to see them work.

- What was it like to work with him? Well, as Heinrich Heine once said, "Ordinarily he was insane, but he had lucid moments when he was merely stupid."

# YOUTH

- He's young, full of good ideas, and always willing to help. And this is what has always made America what it is. As Oscar Wilde reported, "In America, the young are always ready to give to those who are older than themselves the benefit of their inexperience."

- Competing against someone that young is tough. I really understand how Harold L. Ickes felt when he said, "Dewey has thrown his diaper into the ring."

- She's so young, she can't remember what group Paul McCartney was in before Wings.

Have a special roast you've collected or made up? If so, send it to:

**Well-Done Roasts**
c/o St. Martin's Press
175 Fifth Avenue
New York, N.Y. 10010.

We're sorry to say that no compensation or credit can be given, but, if it's appropriate, we'll include it in the next edition of **Well-Done Roasts.**

W.R.E., III & A.F.

# INDEX

151